Work, consumerism and the new poor

ISSUES IN SOCIETY
Series Editor: Tim May

Current and forthcoming titles

Zygmunt Bauman: Work, *Consumerism and the New Poor*
David Byrne: *Social Exclusion*
Graham Crow: *Social Solidarities*
Gerald Delanty: *Citizenship in the Global Age*
Steve Fuller: *The Governance of Science*
Les Johnston: *Crime, Justice and Late Modernity*
Nick Lee: *Childhood and Society*
David Lyon: *Surveillance Society*
Graham Scambler: *Health and Social Change*

Work, consumerism and the new poor

ZYGMUNT BAUMAN

OPEN UNIVERSITY PRESS
Buckingham • Philadelphia

Open University Press
Celtic Court
22 Ballmoor
Buckingham
MK18 1XW

email: enquiries@openup.co.uk
world wide web: http://www.openup.co.uk

and
325 Chestnut Street
Philadelphia, PA 19106, USA

First published 1998
Reprinted 1999

A catalogue record of this book is available from the British Library

ISBN 0 335 20155 5 (pb)   0 335 20156 3 (hb)

Library of Congress Cataloging-in-Publication Data
Bauman, Zygmunt.
        Work, consumerism and the new poor / by Zygmunt Bauman.
            p.   cm. — (Issues in society)
        Includes bibliographical references and index.
        ISBN 0–335–20155–5 (pbk.)   ISBN 0–335–20156–3
        1. Poor. 2. Poor—Public opinion. 3. Work ethic. 4. Consumers—
Attitudes. 5. Production (Economic theory) 6. Public welfare.
I. Title. II. Series.
HC79.P6B36 1998
362.5—dc21   97–47455
                                                          CIP

Typeset by Graphicraft Typesetters Limited, Hong Kong
Printed in Great Britain by Biddles Ltd, Guildford and King's Lynn

Contents

Series editor's foreword

Collectively, the social sciences contribute to a greater understanding of the working of societies and the dynamics of social life. However, they are often not given due credit for this role and much writing has been devoted to why this should be the case. At the same time, we are living in an age in which the role of science in society is being re-evaluated. This has led to both a defence of science as the disinterested pursuit of knowledge and an attack on science as nothing more that an institutionalized assertion of faith with no greater claim to validity than mythology and folklore. These debates tend to generate more heat than light.

In the meantime, the social sciences, in order to remain vibrant and relevant, will reflect the changing nature of these public debates. In so doing, they provide mirrors upon which we gaze in order to understand not only what we have been and what we are now, but to inform ideas about what we might become. This is not simply about understanding the reasons people give for their actions in terms of the contexts in which they act, as well as analysing the relations of cause and effect in the social, political and economic spheres, but about the hopes, wishes and aspirations that people, in their different cultural ways, hold.

In any society that claims to have democratic aspirations, these hopes and wishes are not for the social scientist to prescribe. For this to happen it would mean that the social sciences were able to predict human behaviour with certainty. This would require one theory and one method applicable to all times and places. The physical sciences do not live up to such stringent criteria, while the conditions in societies which provided for this outcome, were it possible, would be intolerable. Why? Because a necessary condition of human freedom is the ability to have acted otherwise and to imagine and practice different ways of organizing societies and living together.

It does not follow from the above that social scientists do not have a valued role to play, as is often assumed in ideological attacks upon their place and function within society. After all, in focusing upon what we have been and what we are now, what we might become is inevitably illuminated. Therefore, while it may not be the province of the social scientist to predict our futures, social scientists are, given not only their understandings, but equal positions as citizens, entitled to engage in public debates concerning future prospects.

This new international series was devised with this general ethos in mind. It seeks to offer students of the social sciences, at all levels, a forum in which ideas are interrogated in terms of their importance for understanding key social issues. This is achieved through a connection between style, structure and content that is found to be both illuminating and challenging in terms of its evaluation of topical social issues, as well as representing an original contribution to the subject under discussion.

Given this underlying philosophy, this series will contain books on topics which are driven by substantive interests. This is not simply a reactive endeavour in terms of reflecting dominant social and political preoccupations, it is also proactive in terms of an examination of issues which relate to and inform the dynamics of social life and the structures of society that are often not part of public discourse. What is distinctive about this series is an interrogation of the assumed characteristics of our current epoch in relation to its consequences for the organization of society and social life, as well as its appropriate mode of study.

Each contribution will contain, for the purposes of general orientation, as opposed to rigid structure, three parts. First, an interrogation of the topic conducted in a manner that renders explicit core assumptions surrounding the issues, and/or an examination of the consequences of historical trends for contemporary social practices. Second, a section which aims to 'bring alive' ideas and practices by considering the ways in which they directly inform the dynamics of social relations. A third section will then move on to make an original contribution to the topic. This will encompass possible future forms and content, likely directions for the study of the phenomena in question, or an original analysis of the topic itself. Of course, it might be a combination of all three.

With the above structure, content and ethos in mind, I am very pleased to be able to launch this series with a contribution to an important social issue by a leading social commentator. Zygmunt Bauman has distinguished himself, through numerous publications, as a leading analyst of contemporary conditions and social practices. His work represents an all too rare combination: a concern to point out the likely consequences of current trends, while refusing to abandon himself to idle speculations concerning the future, accompanied by a methodical, yet passionate, approach to his subject. *Work, Consumerism and the New Poor* is no exception to this. As we devise ever-new policies in the striving to eradicate poverty, one must ask in whose name, with what consequences and for what reasons? When we cease to ask these questions, indifference to the plight of the excluded by the relatively affluent will inevitably result.

Where Zygmunt Bauman is disconcerting for some to read, he is at his most challenging. His analysis refuses to employ those ideas and practices that are characteristic of what many have defined as modernity, as solutions to contemporary problems. Western societies, he argues, are no longer societies of full employment based on the productive capability of labour. As a result, people are now judged in terms of their abilities to be part of the consumer society. No longer seen in terms of productive potential, the poor are excluded on the grounds of being what he terms 'flawed consumers'. This creates new sets of social relations with different consequences for society and the organization of its social policies.

Tracing this history, via the work ethic and changes from production to consumption and its effects on the organization of welfare states, he then looks at the consequences of this for the poor and concludes with a look at possible futures in relation to past and current trends. He writes with an appeal to those who 'have' in their consideration of those who 'have not' and of the indifferences and deafening silences which surrounded the most atrocious acts in history. Thus, a complacent world view is to be guarded against by those who find moral indifference to the plight of the excluded unacceptable.

New solutions, which require a questioning of the ways in which societies are ordered, are needed. Growth for its own sake, without due regard for the overall good of humanity and the forward march of policies which individualize blame for social ills, are not the answer. In contemporary debates over poverty, in which such perspectives are marked by their absence from 'official' deliberations, Zygmunt Bauman's book deserves serious discussion and consideration.

Tim May

Acknowledgements

These go first to Venessa Baird, who enticed me into thinking through the strange twists and turns of the work ethic. Then to Peter Beilharz, who sent me back to the issues with which I tried, years ago, to come to grips in my book *Memories of Class*, but have left unattended since. Then to Claus Offe, who agreed to share with me his vision, insight and knowledge of the subject which I so deeply admire. Last but not least, I thank Tim May, without whose sense of purpose, patience and determination, all my efforts would have been to no avail.

Introduction

The poor will be always with us: this much we can learn from popular wisdom. What popular wisdom is not as confident and outspoken about is the tricky question of how the poor are made to be poor and come to be seen as poor, and how much the way they are made and seen depends on the way we all – ordinary people, neither rich nor poor – live our daily lives and praise or deprecate the fashion in which we and the others live them.

This is a regrettable omission; not just because the poor need and deserve all the attention we may give them, but also because it so happens that it is in the image of the poor that we tend to invest our hidden fears and anxieties, and so looking closely on the way we do this may tell us quite a few important things about our own condition. This book attempts therefore to answer these 'how' questions, and so to tell the often overlooked, glossed over or wilfully concealed part of the story of modern poverty. While attempting to find such answers, it may also add a bit to our self-knowledge.

The poor will be always with us, but what it means to be poor depends on the kind of 'us' they are 'with'. It is not the same to be poor in a society which needs every single adult member to engage in productive labour as it is to be poor in a society which, thanks to the enormous powers accumulated by centuries of labour, may well produce everything needed without the participation of a large and growing section of its members. It is one thing to be poor in a society of producers and universal employment; it is quite a different thing to be poor in a society of consumers, in which life-projects are built around consumer choice rather than work, professional skills, or jobs. If 'being poor' once derived its meaning from the condition of being unemployed, today it draws its meaning primarily from the plight of a flawed consumer. This is one difference which truly makes a difference to the way living in poverty is experienced and to the chances and prospects of redemption from its misery.

This book attempts to trace this change which took place over the duration of modern history, and to make an inventory of its consequences. On the way, it also tries to consider to what extent the well-remembered and tested means of fighting back the advancing poverty and mitigate its hardships are fit (or unfit, as the case may be) to grasp and tackle the problems of poverty in its present form.

The first chapter recalls the origins of the work ethic, which from the beginning of modern times was hoped to attract the poor to regular factory work, to eradicate poverty and assure social peace – all in one go. In practice, it served to train and discipline people, instilling in them the obedience necessary to make the new factory regime work.

The story told in the second chapter is of the gradual yet relentless passage from the early to the later stage of modern society: from a 'society of producers' to a 'society of consumers', and accordingly from a society guided by the work ethic to one ruled by the aesthetic of consumption. In the society of consumers, mass production does not require any more mass labour and so the poor, once a 'reserve army of labour', are re-cast as 'flawed consumers'. This leaves them without a useful social function – actual or potential – with far-reaching consequences for the social standing of the poor and their chances of improvement.

The third chapter traces the rise and fall of the welfare state. It shows the intimate connection between the transformations described in the previous chapter, the sudden emergence of public consensus in favour of collective responsibility for individual misfortune, and the equally abrupt emergence of the present consensus against that principle.

The fourth chapter is concerned with the consequences of all that: a new way in which the poor are socially produced and culturally defined. The recently fashionable concept of the 'underclass' is scrutinized and found to act mainly as a tool of the 'power-assisted' condensation of widely different forms and causes of deprivation into the image of one inferior category of people afflicted with faults common to them all and therefore presenting one 'social problem'.

Finally, the likely futures of the poor and poverty are considered, as well as the possibility of giving the work ethic a new meaning, more relevant to the present condition of developed societies. Can poverty be fought and conquered with the help of orthodox means, made to measure for a society no longer in existence? Or should we seek new solutions, such as the 'decoupling' of the right to livelihood from the selling of labour, and the extension of the socially recognized concept of work beyond that recognized by the labour market? And just how urgent is it to confront such questions and try to find practical answers to them?

PART ONE

The meaning of work: producing the work ethic

What is the work ethic? It is, in a nutshell, one commandment with two outspoken premises and two tacit presumptions.

The first outspoken premise is that in order to get something which one needs to stay alive and happy, one must do something which is seen by others as valuable and worthy of being paid for; there are no 'free lunches', it is always *quid pro quo*, 'tit for tat'; you need to give first, in order to be given later.

The second outspoken premise is that it is wrong – morally mischievous as well as silly – to be satisfied with what one has already got and so to settle for less rather than more; that it is unworthy and unreasonable to stop stretching and straining oneself once what one has seems to be satisfying; that it is undignified to rest, unless one rests in order to gather force for more work. In other words working is a value in its own right, a noble and ennobling activity.

The commandment follows: you should go on working even if you do not see what that could bring you which you do not have already or don't think you need. To work is good, not to work is evil.

The tacit presumption without which neither of these premises nor the commandment would seem as obvious as they do is that most people have their working capacity to sell, and indeed may earn their living selling it and getting what they deserve in exchange; whatever they possess is a reward for their past work and their willingness to go on working. Work is the normal state of all humans; not working is abnormal. Most people fulfil their duty, and it would be unfair to ask them to share their benefits or profits with others, who could also fulfil their duties but for one reason or another fail to do so.

The other tacit presumption is that it is only such labour that has a value recognized by others – labour which commands salaries or wages, which can be sold and is likely to be bought – that has the moral value the work ethic commends. This is, albeit a simple, summary of the form which the work ethic assumed historically in our kind of society, registered under the name of 'modernity'.

Whenever you hear people talking about ethics, you should be pretty sure that someone somewhere is dissatisfied with the way some other people behave and would rather have them behaving differently. Hardly ever has this advice made more sense than in the case of the work ethic.

Since it erupted into the European consciousness in the early stages of industrialization, and in its many avatars throughout the twisted itinerary of modernity and 'modernization', the work ethic served politicians, philosophers and preachers alike as a clarion call to, or an excuse for, attempts to uproot, by hook or by crook, the popular habit which they saw as the prime obstacle to the new brave world they intended to build: the allegedly widespread inclination to avoid, if one could, the ostensible blessings of factory employment, and to resist docile submission to the rhythm of life set by the foreman, the clock and the machine.

The morbid and dangerous habit that the work ethic was meant to fight, destroy and eradicate at the time it entered the public debate, was rooted in the traditional human inclination to consider one's own needs as given and to desire no more than to satisfy them. Once their habitual needs had been met, the 'traditionalist' workers saw no rhyme nor reason to go on working, or for that matter to earn more money; what for, after all? There were so many other interesting and decent things to do, things one could not buy but could well overlook, neglect or lose if one was running after money from dawn to dusk. The threshold of decent life was set low, was fixed and forbidden to cross, and there was no urge to climb higher once that threshold was reached. This is, at any rate, how the entrepreneurs of the time, and the economists who zealously made sense of their troubles, as well as the moral preachers eager to improve things, painted the picture.

Historical memory is held in safe keeping and history is written by victors. No wonder that this composite painting entered the classic canon of history telling, becoming the official record of the valiant battle waged and won by pioneers of modern reason against the irrational, ignorant, totally unreasonable and completely inexcusable popular resistance to progress. According to that record, the stake of the war was to make the blind see light, to force the silly and retarded to use intelligence, and to teach people how to wish for a better life, to desire things new and improved, and by desiring them to self-improve, to become better persons. Or, if need be, to compel the recalcitrant to act as if they had such desires.

As it happened, the true course of events was exactly the opposite to what the early entrepreneurs implied in their complaints against shiftless and laggard factory hands, and what the economists and sociologists took later for the tested truth of history. It was in fact the advent of the factory system that spelled the collapse of the love affair between the craftsman and his work which the 'work ethic' postulated. The moral crusade recorded as the battle for the *introduction* of the work ethic (or as the training in the application of the 'performance principle') was in fact an attempt to *resuscitate* basically pre-industrial work attitudes under new conditions which no longer made them meaningful. The moral crusade aimed at the re-creation, inside the factory under owner-controlled discipline, of the commitment to the wholehearted, dedicated workmanship and the 'state of the art' task performance which once upon a time came to the craftsman naturally when he himself was in control of his work.

Getting people to work

When John Stuart Mill complained that 'we look in vain among the working classes in general for the just pride which will choose to give good work for good wages; for the most part, the sole endeavour is to receive as much and return as little in the shape of service as possible'[1], he bewailed in fact the too rapid conversion of the craftsmen-turned-workers to the market's unemotional, cost-and-effect rationality, and the too fast shedding of the last remnants of pre-modern workmanship instincts. Paradoxically, the appeals to the work ethic seem in this context to cover up the erstwhile drive to *exempt* factory employees from the rule of market rationality which seemed to have a deleterious effect on their dedication to the task. Under the guise of the work ethic, a discipline ethic was promoted: don't mind pride or honour, sense or purpose – work with all your strength, day by day and hour by hour, even if you see no rhyme nor reason to exert yourself and are unable to adumbrate the meaning of the exertion.

The true problem which the pioneers of modernization confronted was the need to force people, used to putting meaning into their work through setting its goals and controlling its course, to expend their skill and their work capacity in the implementation of tasks which were now set and controlled by others and hence meaningless for their performers. The way to solve this problem was a blind drill aimed at habitualizing the workers to an unthinking obedience, while at the same time being denied pride in a job well done and performing a task the sense of which escaped them. As Werner Sombart commented, the new factory system needed part-humans: soulless little wheels in a complex mechanism. The battle was waged against the other, now useless, 'human parts' – human interests and ambitions irrelevant for productive effort and needlessly interfering with the parts deployed in production. The work ethic was, basically, about the surrender of freedom.

That true meaning, which the moral preachings masqueraded as the 'work ethic', had for the people on the receiving end of the crusade, was vividly portrayed in a statement left by an anonymous hosier in 1806:

I found the utmost distaste on the part of the men, to any regular hours or regular habits . . . The men themselves were considerably dissatisfied, because they could not go in and out as they pleased, and have what holidays they pleased, and go on just as they had been used to do; and were subject, during after-hours, to the ill-natured observations of other workmen, to such an extent as completely to disgust them with the whole system, and I was obliged to break it up.[2]

For all intents and purposes, the work-ethic crusade was a battle for control and subordination. It was a power struggle in everything but name, a battle to force the working people to accept, in the name of the ethical nobility of working life, a life neither noble nor responding to their own standards of moral decency.

The crusade was also aimed at detaching things people did from what they saw as worthy of doing and thus as sensible things to do; detaching the work itself from any tangible and understandable purpose it might have served. If fully implemented and absorbed by the logic of life, the work ethic would have replaced all other human activities, such as reflecting, evaluating, choosing and goal-setting, by 'going through the motions'. The motions, moreover, were dictated by rhythms not of one's own making. No wonder that the critics of up-and-coming modernity, in the name of the preservation of what they conceived as the truly human values, spoke in support of the 'right to laziness'.

If implemented, the work ethic would have also separated productive effort from human needs; for the first time in history, it would have given priority to 'what can be done' over the 'what needs to be done'. It would render the satisfaction of human needs irrelevant to the logic, and most importantly to the limits, of productive effort; it would make possible the modern paradox of 'growth for the growth sake'.

. . . a result of the introduction of machinery and of large-scale organisation was the subjection of the workers to a deadening mechanical and administrative routine. Some of the earlier processes of production afforded the workers genuine opportunities for the expression of their personalities in their work, and some of them even permitted the embodiment of artistic conceptions affording pleasure to the craftsmen . . . The anonymous author of *An Authentic Account of the Riots of Birmingham* (1799) explains the participation of workers in the riots by saying that the nature of their employments is such that 'they are taught to act, not to think'.[3]

In the poignant summary by J.L. and Barbara Hammonds:

the upper classes allowed no values to the workpeople but those which the slave-owner appreciates in the slave. The working man was to be industrious and attentive, not to think for himself, to owe loyalty and attachment to his master alone, to recognise that his proper place in the economy of the state was the place of the slave in the economy of the sugar plantation. Take many virtues we admire in a man, and they become vices in a slave.[4]

Indeed, in the chorus of exhortations to submit, placidly and unthinkingly, to the impersonal, inhuman and mechanical rhythm of factory work, there was a curious blend of such an essentially pre-industrial and anti-modern mentality of slave economy and the new bold vision of the wonderful, miraculously plentiful world which once the fetters of traditional ways were broken was bound to emerge as a result of human invention, and above all of human mastery over nature.

As Wolf Lepenies observed, the language in which 'nature' (that is, all things already shaped through divine creation, things 'given', unprocessed and untouched by human reason and skills) was talked about from the end of the seventeenth century on was saturated with military concepts and metaphors.[5] Francis Bacon left nothing to the imagination: nature ought to be conquered and set to work hard so that it could serve human interests and comfort better than it ever could when left alone. Descartes compared the progress of reason to a string of victorious battles waged against nature, while Diderot called the practitioners and the theorists to unite in the name of the conquest and subjugation of nature; Karl Marx defined historical progress as the unstoppable march towards human dominion over nature. No difference of opinion here, whatever their other disagreements, with Claude Saint-Simon or August Comte.

Once the ultimate goal had been spelled out, the sole significance ascribed to practical undertakings was the shortening of the distance which still separated people of the time from the final triumph over nature. The authority of other criteria could be successfully contested and gradually yet relentlessly rendered null and void. Among the progressively dismissed criteria of evaluation, the precepts of pity, compassion and care figured most prominently. Pity for the victims weakened the resolve, made the compassionate slow down the pace of change, and whatever arrested or slackened progress could not be moral. On the other hand, whatever served the ultimate conquest of nature was good and 'in the last account' ethical, serving 'in the long run' the improvement of mankind. The craftsmen's defence of their traditional rights, the resistance to the rational, effective and efficient regime of mechanized work which the pre-industrial poor had shown, were seen as another obstacle among the many which nature in its bland stupor had stood in the way of progress as if to stave off its imminent defeat. That resistance had to be broken with as little compunction as all nature's other shrewd contrivances had already been broken, debunked and defused, or merely swept out of the way.

The leading lights of the glorious world which was to be built with human wits and skills – the designers of machines and the pioneers of their use – had no doubts that the real carriers of progress were the creative minds of the inventors. James Watt argued in 1785 that all the others, whose physical exertion was needed to make the inventors' ideas into flesh, 'are to be considered in no other light than as mere acting mechanical powers . . . it is scarcely necessary that they should use their reason'.[6] While Richard Arkwright complained that it was difficult to train human beings 'to renounce their desultory habits of work, and identify themselves with the unvarying regularity of the complex automaton'. To be efficiently used, the complex automaton required to be constantly watched; and few countrymen or women relished the idea of spending ten or more hours a day shut up in a factory watching a machine.

Their resistance to join in the concerted effort of humanity was itself the oft quoted proof of the moral laxity of the poor and the moral virtue of a tough and rigid, no-punches-held factory discipline. Getting the poor and 'voluntarily idle' to work was not just an economic, but a moral task. The enlightened opinions of the time, differing as they might have been from each other in all other respects, had little to quarrel about on this point. *Blackwood's Magazine* wrote that 'the influence by the master over the man, is of itself a point gained in the direction of moral improvement'[7], while the *Edinburgh Review* acidly remarked, about the ongoing cultural crusade, that:

> it is not in [the charity] spirit that the new schemes of benevolence are conceived . . . They are celebrated as the beginning of a new moral order . . . in which the possessors of property are to resume their place as the paternal guardians of those less fortunate . . . to extinguish, not indeed poverty – that hardly seems to be thought desirable – but the more abject forms of vice, destitution, and physical wretchedness.[8]

P. Gaskell, the author and social activist who went down in history as one of the most philanthropic, warm-hearted and compassionate friends of the poor, held, despite this, little doubt that the objects of his compassion 'differ but little in inherent qualities from the uncultivated child of nature'[9] and that they needed other, more mature people to watch their moves and take responsibility for their actions. Among the contributors to the learned opinion the agreement was common that the present or would-be labourers were not capable of managing their lives on their own. No more than silly, unruly children were they able to govern themselves, to tell what was right and what was wrong, what was good for them and what harmful, let alone to see what might prove in the long run to be 'in their best interest'. They were but a raw human material to be processed and given the right shape; at least for some considerable time to come they were bound to remain on the receiving end of social change – to be the objects, not the subjects, of the ongoing rational overhaul of human society. The work ethic was one of the pivotal items on the sweeping moral/educational agenda, and the tasks it set for the men of thought and action alike constituted the core of what came to be dubbed later by the eulogists of modern departures the 'civilizing process'.

Like every other set of ethical precepts for proper, decent, meritorious conduct, the work ethic was simultaneously a constructive vision and a prescription for a demolishing job. It denied legitimacy to the habits, preferences or desires entertained by the human targets of the ethical crusade. It painted the pattern for the right kind of behaviour, but above all it cast suspicion upon everything that the people earmarked for ethical training might have been doing while unschooled and unforced. Their inclinations could not be trusted; free to act as they wished and left to their own whims or predilections, they would rather starve than make an effort, wallow in filth rather than care about self-improvement, put a momentary, ephemeric diversion above more distant yet steady happiness, and all in all prefer doing nothing to doing work. All these morbid, uncontrolled impulses were part of the 'tradition' the emerging industry had to stand up to, fight against, and in the end exterminate. As Max Weber (in Michael Rose's apt summary) was to point out, looking back on the job already performed, the work ethic 'amounted to an attack' on the 'traditionalism of ordinary workers' who 'had operated with a fixed image of their material needs which led them to prefer leisure and to forego opportunities to increase their income by working harder or longer'. Traditionalism 'was disparaged'.[10]

Indeed, for the pioneers of the brave new world of modernity, 'tradition' was a dirty word. It stood for the morally disgraceful and condemnable inclinations that the work ethic rose up against: the inclinations of the creatures of habit to settle today for what they had yesterday, for eschewing 'the more' and neglecting the better if getting it called for an extra effort (in fact, for surrendering to a crude, cruel, off-putting and incomprehensible, alien regime). The officially-named enemies in the war declared by the work ethic against the 'traditionalism' of the pre-industrial poor were ostensibly the modesty of human needs and the mediocrity of human wants. The actual battles – most ferocious and merciless battles – were waged against the reluctance of would-be factory hands to suffer the discomfort and indignity of a work regime they neither desired nor understood, and most certainly would not have chosen by their own volition.

Work or perish

The work ethic was meant to kill two birds with one stone: resolve the labour-supply problems of burgeoning industry, and dispose of one of the most vexing nuisances the post-traditional society had to encounter – the necessity to provide for the needs of those who for one reason or another could not catch up with the change of circumstances, make ends meet and eke out their own existence under the new conditions. Not everyone could be pushed through the treadmills of factory labour; there were invalids, the weak, sick and old who by no stretch of imagination could be envisaged as coping with the harsh demands of industrial employment. Brian Inglis portrayed the mood of the time:

the case gained ground that the destitute were expendable, whether or not they were to blame for their condition. Had there been any way simply to get rid of them, without risk to society, Ricardo and Malthus would certainly have recommended it, and governments would equally certainly have given it their favourable attention, provided that it did not entail any increase in taxation.[11]

But no such method 'simply to get rid of them' was available, and in its absence another, less perfect, solution needed to be found. The precept of work – any work, on any condition – as the sole decent, morally passable way of gaining one's right to live went a long way towards finding it. No one spelled out this 'second best' strategy in more blunt and candid terms than Thomas Carlyle in his 1837 essay on Chartism:

> If paupers are made miserable, paupers will needs decline in multitude. It is a secret known to all rat-catchers: stop up the granary-crevices, afflict with continual mewing, alarm, and going-off of traps, your 'chargeable labourers' disappear, and cease from the establishment. A still briefer method is that of arsenic; perhaps even a milder, where otherwise permissible.

Gertrude Himmelfarb, in her monumental study of the idea of poverty, unpacks this view in the following fashion:

> Paupers, like rats, could indeed be eliminated by this method, or at least driven out of sight. All that was required was the determination to treat them like rats, on the assumption that the 'poor and luckless are here only as a nuisance to be abraded and abated'.[12]

In the efforts to cause the paupers to 'decline in multitude' the contribution of the work ethic was indeed priceless. That ethic asserted, after all, the moral superiority of any kind of life, however miserable, providing it was supported by the wages of labour. Armed with such an ethical canon, the well-wishing reformers could proclaim the principle of 'less eligibility' of all 'unearned' assistance which society might have offered its poor, and consider that principle a deeply moral step towards a more humane society. 'Less eligibility' meant that the conditions purveyed to people relying on relief instead of wages must make their life yet less attractive than the life of the poorest and the most wretched among the hired labourers. It was hoped that the more the life of the non-working poor were degraded and the deeper they descended into destitution, the more tempting or at least the less unendurable would appear to them the lot of those working poor who had sold their labour in exchange for the most miserable of wages; and so the cause of the work ethic would be helped and its triumph brought nearer.

These and similar considerations must have been high in the minds of the 'Poor Law' reformers of the 1820s and 1830s, who after protracted and at times acrimonious debate came to a virtually unanimous decision to confine all the available assistance to the indigent part of the population (the part which Jeremy Bentham preferred to call the 'refuse' or the 'dross' of the population) to the *inside* of the poorhouses. This decision had a number of advantages, as far as the advancing of the work-ethic's cause was concerned.

First and foremost, it sorted out the 'true paupers' from those who were

suspected of merely masquerading as such in order to avoid the discom-
forts of regular work. No one but the 'true pauper' would choose confinement to the poorhouse if the conditions inside were made sufficiently
horrifying. The limitation of assistance to such as could be obtained in the
drab and squalid interior of the poorhouse made the 'means test' redundant, or rather self-administered by the poor themselves: whoever agreed to
be locked up inside a poorhouse must indeed have had no other way of
staying alive.

Second, the abolition of outside assistance made the poor think twice
before deciding that the requirements of the work ethic were 'not for them',
that they could not cope with what regular work demands, or that the
stern and in many ways abhorrent demands of factory work were a choice
worse than its alternative; even the most niggardly wages and the most
gruelling and tedious drudgery on the factory floor would appear bearable
– even desirable – in comparison.

The principles of the new Poor Law also set a clear and 'objective' dividing line between those who could be reformed and converted to abide by
the precepts of the work ethic, and those who were fully and truly beyond
redemption and from whom no service for the benefit of society could be
squeezed, however ingenious or unscrupulous were the measures taken.

Finally, the Poor Law guarded the working (or potentially working)
poor from contamination by the hopelessly idle, separating them from
trouble with the help of massive, impenetrable walls, soon to be duplic-
ated by the invisible, yet no less tangible for that reason, walls of cultural
estrangement. The more terrifying the news leaked from behind the poorhouse walls, the more the slavery of factory hands would look like freedom
and their wretchedness like a stroke of luck and a blessing.

It can be guessed from what has been said so far that the project of
sorting out once and for all the 'true paupers' from the merely pretending,
malingering and counterfeit ones, and so setting apart the hopeless from the
hopeful objects of working drill in order to stave off the danger of morally
morbid contamination, was never to succeed in full. The poor of the two
legally distinguished categories of 'deserving' and 'undeserving' did influence
each other a lot, though not necessarily in the fashion which the reformers
declared to be the main reason for the construction of poorhouses.

True, the establishment of new and particularly appalling and repulsive
conditions for those who had been administered the plight of the paupers
(or, as the reformers preferred to say, 'had chosen' it) made the poor more
receptive to the doubtful attractions of hired labour and so warded off the
much publicized threat of contaminating them with idleness, but it *did*
contaminate them with poverty, and so contributed heavily to the perpetuation of the same bane which the work ethic was meant, once triumphant,
to eliminate. The dreadful ugliness of poorhouse existence, which served as
the reference point for assessing the quality of factory life, lowered further
the depths to which employers could push their employees' endurance without fear of either rebellion or withdrawal of labour. In the end, there was

little to distinguish between the lot of those who embraced the instructions of the work ethic and those who refused to do so or had fallen by the way-side while trying to embrace it and to live according to its commandments.

The most insightful, sceptical or cynical among the moral reformers of early modernity did not in any case entertain the illusion that the theor-etically elegant distinction between the two – genuine and pretending – categories of the poor could be expressed in two distinct strategies. Nor did they believe that such bifurcation of strategy would make much practical sense either in terms of economy of resources or in the form of a tangible ethical benefit.

Notably, Jeremy Bentham made no distinction between the regimes of 'houses of industry': workhouses, poorhouses and manufactories (as well as prisons, lunatic asylums, hospitals and schools, for that matter).[13] Whatever their ostensible purpose, he insisted, all faced the same practical problem and shared the same concerns: all of them had to impose one, uniform pattern of regular and predictable behaviour upon a variegated and essentially unruly population of inmates. All of them, in a nutshell, had to neutralize or cancel out the variety of human habits and inclinations so that one standard of con-duct could be attained for all. The same task confronted the supervisors of industrial plants and the wardens of poorhouses. In order to obtain what they desired – a disciplined, repetitive routine – both kinds of inmates, the 'working' and 'non-working' poor alike, had to be subjected to an identical regime. No wonder that the differences in moral quality of the two categor-ies, given such close attention and assigned such a crucial importance in the arguments of the ethical preachers and reformers, hardly ever appear in Bentham's reasoning. After all, the hub of his strategy was precisely to render such differences totally irrelevant to the stated purpose, and sufficiently impotent so as not to interfere with the outcome.

In taking such a stance, Bentham spoke in unison with the economic wisdom of his times. As John Stuart Mill was to write shortly after, polit-ical economy is not interested in human passions and motives, 'except those which may be regarded as perpetually antagonizing principles to the desire for wealth, namely aversion to labour, and desire of the present enjoyment of costly indulgencies'.[14] Like all scholars searching for the 'objective', impersonal, will-independent laws of economic life, Bentham stripped the task of promoting the new social order of evangelical adornments so com-mon in the work ethic debate right down to its hard core, which was the entrenchment of routine regular behaviour based on unconditional disci-pline aided and guarded by effective supervision from top to bottom. He had no time for worries about spiritual enlightenment or mind reform; he did not expect the inmates of a panopticon-like establishment to love their work (he took their incurable aversion to work virtually for granted) and did not bother to eulogize over the work's morally ennobling impact. If the inmates were to behave in line with the precepts of the work ethic, this could happen not so much thanks to their moral conversion, but to their being cast in a situation of no choice, one containing no alternative to acting *as if* the commandments of the work ethic had been embraced and absorbed into their consciences. Bentham did not vest his hopes in the cultivation of the choosers' virtues, but in the simplicity of the choice they faced, or the complete absence of all choice. In the panopticon, be it a poorhouse, a workhouse or a factory, 'if a man won't work nothing has he to do, from morning to night, but to eat his bad bread and drink his water, without a soul to speak to . . . This encouragement is necessary to his doing his utmost; but more than this is not necessary'.

Promotion of the work ethic inspired a lot of preaching from the church pulpits, the composition of many moralizing tales, and the mushrooming of Sunday schools which did their best to fill young heads with the right rules and values; but for all the practical intents and purposes it boiled down – as Bentham with his characteristic straightforwardness and sobriety of mind revealed – to the radical reduction of choice that the present and the intended factory hands were facing. The principle of no relief outside the poorhouse was one manifestation of the thrust to establish the 'no-choice' situation. The other manifestation of the same strategy was the induction of the hand-to-mouth existence – keeping wages at a level low enough to allow for no more than physical survival until the dawn of the next day of hard work, and so make another day of hard work a 'no choice', a necessity.

Both expedients entailed, though, an element of risk, since in the end they appealed willy-nilly to the rational faculties of their objects, in however demeaned a version: to be effective, both needed thinking, calculating persons at the receiving end. But thinking could be a double-edged sword; or, rather, a dangerous crevice left in an otherwise tight wall, through which troublesome, unpredictable and incalculable factors such as the human passion for dignified life or a motivation towards self-assertion, could crawl back from enforced exile. An additional insurance needed to be taken up, and none promised more security than physical coercion. Corporal punishment, cutting the wages or food supply below the subsistence level, and above all a continuous and ubiquitous surveillance and prompt penalty for the violation of any, however trivial, rule, could be trusted to bring the plight of the poor yet closer to the situation of no choice.

This made the preaching of the work ethic look suspiciously duplicitous. Indeed, counting on moral integrity of the human objects of industrial drill would have to entail the expanding of their realm of freedom – the only soil in which moral selves can grow and moral responsibilities can come to fruition. But the work ethic, in its early history at least, opted for the cutting down, or a complete elimination of, choice.

Duplicity was not necessarily intended, nor always conscious. There is reason to suppose that the promoters of the work ethic were indifferent to the moral consequences of their actions, let alone that they were immoral themselves. The cruelty of the proposed and applied measures was honestly viewed as an indispensable part of a moral crusade, itself a powerful moralizing agent and so by itself a highly moral act. Hard work was praised as an uplifting experience – a spiritual enhancement which could be achieved only by the all-brakes-released service of the common good. If inducing people to hard work and making hard work their habit called for the affliction of pain, then this was a reasonable price to pay for future gains, not least for the moral benefits which the life of hard work would secure. As Keith McClelland pointed out, if 'manual work was seen by many as a necessary, burdening, compulsion', it was 'also seen as an activity to be celebrated'[15], on account of the honour and wealth it would bring to the nation, and not least for the moral improvement it would bestow upon the workers themselves.

Producing the producers

Societies tend to hold an idealized view of themselves which allows them to 'keep on course': to spot and locate the scars, warts, and other blemishes spoiling their present look, as well as to conceive of a remedy sure to heal or smooth them up. Going to work – taking up employment, having a master, doing things which the master must have considered useful since he is prepared to pay to have them done – was thus the way to become a decent human fellow for all those whose decency or indeed humanity had not been assured in any other way, was doubted and had yet to be proved. Giving work to all and making all into workers was commonly seen as the recipe for all ills and troubles society might have endured because of its (transitory, as it was hoped) imperfection or immaturity.

Neither on the right nor on the left of the political spectrum was this historical role of work questioned. The dawning realization of living in an 'industrial society' went hand in hand with the conviction and the confidence that the number of people transformed into industrial workers was bound to grow unstoppably and that the ultimate shape the industrial society was obliged to assume would be a sort of gigantic factory, in which every able-bodied male was productively employed. Universal employment was the norm not-yet-fully-met, but represented the shape of things to come. In the light of that norm, being out of work appeared as *un*employment, *ab*normality, a breach of the norm. 'Get to work' and 'get people to work' were the twin exhortations/conjurations that it was hoped would put paid simultaneously to personal troubles and shared, social ills. These were *modern* slogans, reverberating on both sides of the great divide which was to separate the capitalist and the communist versions of modernity. The war cry of the Marxist-inspired opposition to capitalism was 'who does not work, does not eat', and the vision of the classless society to come was that of a society built in all its aspects after the likeness of a factory. In that classic era of modern industrial society, work was simultaneously the pivot of individual life, social order and the survival capacity ('systemic reproduction') of society as a whole.

To start with individual life. The work a man performed supplied his livelihood; but the *kind* of work performed defined the standing a man could reasonably hope for or claim inside his immediate neighbourhood and in that imagined totality called 'society'. Work was the main factor of one's social placement as well as of self-assessment: for all people except those who thanks to hereditary or acquired wealth could combine a life of leisure with self-sufficiency, the question 'who are you' was answered by pointing to the company by which the asked man was employed and the capacity in which he was employed by it. In a society known for its knack and fondness for categorizing and classifying, the type of work was the decisive, pivotal classification from which everything else relevant to living among others followed. It defined a man's equals, to whom he could compare himself and orient himself with, his superiors, to whom he owed respect, and those lower down, from whom he was entitled to expect or demand deference. The type of work defined the life standards which one should match and obey, the kind of Joneses to which one ought to 'live up to' and other Joneses one should steer clear of in social life. The work career marked the itinerary of life and retrospectively provided the prime record of one's life achievement or one's failure; that career was the principal source of self-confidence and uncertainty, self-satisfaction and self-reprobation, pride amd shame.

In other words, for the large and growing majority of males in post-traditional, modern society – a society which assessed and rewarded its members on the assumption of their capacity for choice and the duty of self-assertion – work stood at the centre of the lifelong construction and defence of a man's identity. The life-project could spring from many ambitions, but they were all wrapped around the type of work to be chosen or be assigned to. The type of work coloured the totality of life; it determined not just the rights and duties directly relevant to the work process, but the expected standard of living, the pattern of the family, social life and leisure, norms of propriety and daily routine. It was that one 'independent variable' which allowed a person to shape up and to forecast, with little error, all other aspects of their existence. Once the type of work had been decided and the scheme of career ascribed, all the rest fell into place and one could be pretty certain what was to be done in virtually every field of life. To sum up: work was the main orientation point, in reference to which all other life pursuits could be planned and ordered.

As to the role of the work ethic in the regulation of social order, since most of the male members of modern society in its industrial phase spent most of their waking hours and most years of their mature life at work (according to Roger Sue's calculations, 70 per cent of waking life was on average taken up by work in 1850[16]), the workplace was the primary site of social integration; the setting in which the essential habits of obedience to norms and of disciplined behaviour were expected to be trained and absorbed and in which the 'social character' was to be formed – at least in all its aspects relevant to the perpetuation of an orderly society. Alongside the mass conscript army, another of the great modern inventions, the factory was the main 'panoptical institution' of modern society.

Factories turned out many and varied commodities, but all of them, in addition, produced the compliant and conforming subjects of the modern state. This second though by no means subsidiary productive line, albeit less salient and less talked about, secured for industrial work a function more basic for society's survival than one might deduce from the work's ostensible role – that of the production of material wealth. Just how crucial that other, latent function was, one can gather from the panics which periodically erupted throughout the modern era whenever the news broke out that a considerable part of the adult population was physically unfit for regular factory employment and/or army service. Whatever explicit reasons were given to justify the concern, invalidity, weakness of the body and mental impairment were seen as a threat and were feared because they cast their victims outside the reach of the panoptical drill on which the maintenance of social order relied; people out of employment were also masterless people, people out of control – not surveilled, not monitored, not subjected to any regular, sanctions-fortified, routine. No wonder that the model of health developed during the nineteenth century by socially-conscious medical sciences was that of a male capable of the kind of physical exertion required by factory work and military service.

If the subjection of the bulk of the male population to the drilling impact of factory work was the principal method of production and maintenance of social order, the strong and stable patriarchal family with the employed ('bread providing') male as its absolute, uncontested ruler was its necessary supplement; not by chance the preachers of work ethics were as a rule also the advocates of family virtues and the unshakable rights and duties of the family heads. Inside the family, husbands/fathers were prompted to perform the same surveilling/disciplining role towards womenfolk and children as factory foremen and army sergeants performed in relation to them on the factory floor or on the exercise range. Modern disciplining power, as Foucault insisted, was dispersed and distributed after the pattern of capillary vessels which conduct the blood pumped by the heart to the most distant tissues and cells of a living organism. The husband/father's authority inside the family conducted the disciplining pressures of the order-producing and order-servicing network to the parts of the population which the panoptical institutions would not be otherwise able to reach.

Finally, a decisive role was allotted to work in what the politicians habitually presented as the question of society's survival and prosperity, and what made its way into sociological discourse under the name of 'systemic reproduction'. The substance of modern industrial society was the reprocessing of natural resources with the help of (again natural) supplies of workable energy, 'wealth' being the outcome of that reprocessing. Such reprocessing was organized under the auspices of the owners/managers of capital, but achieved through the application of hired labour. The continuity of that reprocessing depended therefore on the owners of the capital successfully engaging the rest of the population in the role of producers.

The volume of product, utilized as the essential resource in the expansion of wealth, depended on the direct involvement of 'living labour' in the productive effort and its subordination to that effort's logic; productive roles were the essential units of the system. The coercive powers of governments were used primarily to make this possible – that is, for the purpose of 'commodification' of capital and labour. In other words, for realizing the potential of wealth as *capital* (i.e. such wealth as can be used to produce more wealth), and of individual members of society as the 'value-adding' labour. The growth of active capital and employment were the main issues of politics. The successes or failures of policies were measured by the extent to which that task had been fulfilled: by the hiring powers of the capital and the extent of engagement of the population in the process of production.

To sum up: work occupied the focal position on all three analytically distinguishable levels of modern arrangement – individual, social and systemic. In addition, work served as a linchpin bringing the three levels together, and as the main factor through which communication and coordination between the three levels was negotiated, achieved and preserved.

The work ethic was thus crucially instrumental in bringing the modern arrangement about. The mutual engagement of capital and labour indispensable for the daily functioning and perpetuation of modern industrial society were presented by the work ethic as the moral duty, mission and vocation of all its members (more exactly, all its male members); the work ethic called men to embrace willingly, gladly, enthusiastically, what was in fact an unavoidable necessity – a plight which the practitioners of the new economy, aided and abetted by the legislators of the new state, did their best to render inescapable. But to embrace that necessity willingly meant giving up all resistance to rules experienced as an alien and painful imposition. In the workplace, autonomy of workers was not tolerated. The work ethic called people to *choose* a life devoted to labour; but a life devoted to labour meant no choice, inaccesibility of choice and prohibition of choice.

From 'better' to 'more'

The precepts of the work ethic were preached with a zeal proportional to the resistance of the would-be labourers to their loss of freedom. Preaching was aimed at overcoming that resistance. The work ethic was an instrument, while the end that instrument was to bring closer was the compliance with the factory regime and the loss of independence it entailed.

Instrumental reason allows all means to be chosen, critically assessed and – if need be – discarded and replaced according to their effectiveness in bringing the desired result about. The work ethic, and more generally the appeal to the sentiments and the consciences of the current and would-be factory workers, was but one of several alternative means of making the wheels of the industrial system turn. It was not necessarily the most efficient one, and certainly not the only one conceivable. Neither was it the most reliable; work morality which the preachers of the work ethic sought to instil was likely to remain, like all morality, fickle and erratic – a poor guide to expected human behaviour and a pressure not steady enough to match the strict, unyielding and monotonous work effort required by the factory routine. The latter could not rely on moral sentiments, on appeals to moral responsibility (and so in the end to *choice*), for securing the immutable rhythm of physical exertion and unqualified obedience to the work regime.

We have already noted that when addressed to the poor and indolent the preaching of the work ethic went hand in hand with resorting to more reliable means of pressure, like compulsory confinement, legal bonding, refusal of all relief except that available inside the poorhouses, ending with the threat of corporal punishment. The *preaching* of the work ethic called for moral choice; the *practice* of work reduced or eliminated the choice altogether, striving to make sure that its objects would behave as if they have been converted whether the conversion was sincere or not, whether the work ethic's gospel was believed or not. The general trend in the modern organizations, which the modern factories shared, was towards rendering the moral sentiments of human agents *irrelevant* to their actions ('adiaphoric') so that those actions were regular and predictable to an extent which notoriously non-rational moral impulses would never be counted on to reach.

The work ethic seems to be a mainly European invention; most American social historians agree that it was the spirit of enterprise and the desire for upward mobility, rather than the work ethic, that lubricated the wheels of American industry. Work, dedicated work, and ever more dedicated work, was seen almost from the beginning by both the immigrant and the American-born workers as a means rather than a value in its own right, a way of life or a vocation: the means to get richer, and so more independent; the means to get rid of the repulsive necessity to work for others. Even the semi-slavery of sweatshops was accepted and placidly endured in the name of future freedom, without any pretence as to its ennobling quality. Work did not need to be loved or believed to be the sign of moral virtue; it could be openly resented without incurring the risk of the collapse of discipline, as long as bearing with even the most horrid conditions was seen as a price temporarily paid for the happiness of freedom never too far away.

In Michael Rose's opinion[17], the trend to disregard and push aside the ethics of work deepened in America and acquired a new speed at the dawn of the twentieth century; main managerial innovations which gained popularity by that time operated 'in such a way as to destroy moral commitment to work effort. But they took on the character they did, it seems likely, because moral commitment to work effort was generally undependable' – or so it was seen in the acquisitive atmosphere of the land of riches and enrichment. The overall tendency culminated in the scientific management movement initiated by Frederick Winslow Taylor:

Appeal to a Work Ethic played virtually no part in his package of management techniques. Positive work commitment was encouraged primarily through carefully manipulated money incentives. Taylor's model labourer was not a native-born American, but a Dutch immigrant, a certain Schmidt. What fascinated Taylor in Schmidt was certainly not any sense of moral obligation on Schmidt's part to work effectively and ingeniously, but his excitable response to the sight of a dollar bill and his willingness to do whatever Taylor told him to do in order to get his hands on it.

Not counting on the labourers' belief in the intrinsically ennobling quality of work was a sensible choice, as inequality of human conditions grew more and more salient and the pressure of the incapacitating factory discipline ever more merciless. And yet the advantages of playing down the promise of the American Dream – that all factory-floor sufferings would prove in the end but a temporary nuisance and that the surrender to the whims of the bosses was but a means to become a boss in one's own right – became also increasingly obvious. After all, the chance to firm up one's feet enough to stand on them became increasingly vague and remote, and the passages leading from manual labour to the freedoms of 'working on one's own account' shrunk and clotted. Independence of the work effort from moral commitment to work and from the elevated views of the virtues of working life had to be secured by other means.

Another means was found, in America as well as elsewhere, in the 'material incentives to work': rewards attached to the obedient acceptance of factory discipline and so to the renunciation of the worker's independence. What had been achieved with sermons, aided or not by the threat of a stick, was more and more often sought through the seductive powers of a carrot. Rather than asserting that work effort is a road to a morally superior way of life, it was now to be advertised as a means to *earn more money*. Do not mind the 'better', the 'more' is the sole thing that counts.

What was at the start of industrial society a power conflict, a fight for autonomy and freedom, has been gradually yet relentlessly channelled into the struggle for a greater share of the surplus while tacitly accepting the extant power structure and striking its rectification out from the agenda. Increasingly, it was the ability to win a greater share of the surplus that came to be seen as the definitive way to restore that human dignity which was lost when the craftsmen turned into factory hands. Appeals to the morally ennobling capacity of the work effort fell, in the process, by the board. It was now wage differentials, not the genuine or putative virtues or vices of keen dedication or a lukewarm attitude to work, that measured the prestige and social standing of the producers.

The fact that the power conflict about the quality of social existence was channelled into the struggle for the quantity of monetary income and that economic gains became the sole expression of the ambitions to autonomy and self-assertion, has had a profound influence on the whole course of development of modern, industrial society. It elicited the kind of conduct which the original work ethic, supported by the means of economic and occasionally physical coercion, strove to achieve in vain. It instilled in the minds and the actions of modern producers not so much the 'spirit of capitalism' as the tendency to assess human value and dignity in terms of monetary rewards. It also shifted human motivation and the craving for freedom firmly and thus irretrievably into the sphere of consumption. These effects came to determine in large measure the later history of modern society as it moved from a society of producers to that of consumers.

This latter path was not followed in the same measure or with the same consequences in all branches of modern society. Though a mixture of coercion and possessive stimuli was used to assure the obedience to the work ethic in all parts of the modern world, the ingredients were blended in different proportions. Most notably, the appeal to the consumer hiding in the producer was to remain inconsistent, half-hearted and unconvincing in the communist version of modern society. It was for that reason among others that the hiatus between the two versions of modernity grew in time ever deeper, and that the ascent of consumerism which profoundly transformed the modality of life in the West made the communist regime awestruck, and found it totally unprepared, unable to catch up, and ever more inclined to cut its losses, admit its inferiority and throw in the towel.

From the work ethic to the aesthetic of consumption

Ours is a consumer society.

We all know, more or less, what it means to be a 'consumer'. A consumer is a person who consumes, and to consume means using things up: eating them, wearing them, playing with them and otherwise causing them to satisfy one's needs or desires. Since in our part of the world it is money which in most cases 'mediates' between desire and its satisfaction, being a consumer also means – normally means – *appropriating* most of the things destined to be consumed: buying them, paying for them and so making them one's exclusive property, barring everybody else from using them without the one's permission.

To consume also means to destroy. In the course of consumption, the consumed things cease to exist, literally or spiritually. Either they are 'used up' physically to the point of complete annihilation, such as when things are eaten or worn out, or they are stripped of their allure, no longer arouse and attract desire, and forfeit their capacity to satisfy one's needs and wishes – for example, an overused toy or an overplayed record – and so become unfit for consumption.

This is what being a consumer means, but what do we mean when we speak of a consumer society? Is there something special about being a consumer in a consumer society? And besides, is not every known society a society of consumers, to a greater or lesser extent? All the features listed in the preceding paragraph, except perhaps the need to pay money for things meant to be consumed, are surely present in any kind of society. Of course, what sort of objects we see as the potential stuff of consumption, and how we consume them, may differ from time to time and from one place to another, but no human being anywhere or at any time can stay alive without consuming.

And so when we say that ours is a 'consumer society' we must have in mind something more than the trivial, ordinary and not particularly illuminating fact that all members of that society consume. Ours is a 'consumer society' in a similarly profound and fundamental sense in which the society of our predecessors (modern society in its industrial phase described in the previous chapter) used to deserve the name of a 'producer society' in spite of the fact that people have produced since the beginning of the human species and will go on producing until the species' demise. The reason for calling that older type of modern society a 'producer society' was that it engaged its members *primarily* as producers; the way in which that society shaped up its members was dictated by the need to play this role and the norm that society held up to its members was the ability and the willingness to play it. In its present late-modern, second-modern or post-modern stage, society engages its members – again *primarily* – in their capacity as consumers. The way present-day society shapes up its members is dictated first and foremost by the need to play the role of the consumer, and the norm our society holds up to its members is that of the ability and willingness to play it.

The difference between then and now is not as radical as abandoning one role and replacing it with another. Neither of the two societies could do without at least some of its members taking charge of producing things to be consumed, and all members of both societies do, of course, consume. The difference is one of emphasis, but that shift of emphasis does make an enormous difference to virtually every aspect of society, culture and individual life. The differences are so deep and ubiquitous that they fully justify speaking of our society as a society of a separate and distinct kind – a consumer society.

The passage from producer to consumer society has entailed many profound changes; arguably the most decisive among them is, however, the fashion in which people are groomed and trained to meet the demands of their social identities (that is, the fashion in which men and women are 'integrated' into the social order and given a place in it). Panoptical institutions, once crucial in that respect, have fallen progressively out of use. With mass industrial employment fast shrinking and universal military duty replaced with small, voluntary and professional armies, the bulk of the population is unlikely ever to come under their direct influence. Technological progress has reached the point where productivity grows together with the tapering of employment; factory crews get leaner and slimmer; 'downsizing' is the new principle of modernization. As the editor of the *Financial Times* Martin Wolf calculates, between 1970 and 1994 the proportion of people employed in industry fell from 30 per cent to 20 per cent in the European Union and from 28 per cent to 16 per cent in the USA, while industrial productivity progressed on average by 2.5 per cent per annum.[1]

The kind of drill in which the panoptical institutions excelled is hardly suitable for the training of consumers. Those institutions were good at training people in routine, monotonous behaviour, and reached that effect through the limitation or complete elimination of choice; but it is precisely the absence of routine and the state of constant choice that are the virtues (indeed, the 'role prerequisites') of a consumer. And so, in addition to being much reduced in the post-industrial and post-conscription world, the panoptical drill is also irreconcilable with the needs of a consumer society. The qualities of temperament and life attitudes which the panoptical drill excels in cultivating are counter-productive in the production of ideal consumers.

Ideally, acquired habits should lie on the shoulders of the consumers just like the religiously/ethically inspired vocational and acquisitive passions used to lie, as Max Weber repeated after Baxter, on the shoulders of the protestant saint: 'like a light cloak, ready to be thrown aside at any moment'.[2] And habits are indeed continually, daily, at the first opportunity thrown aside, never given the chance to solidify into the iron bars of a cage. Ideally, nothing should be embraced by a consumer firmly, nothing should command a commitment forever, no needs should be ever seen as fully satisfied, no desires considered ultimate. There ought to be a proviso 'until further notice' attached to any oath of loyalty and any commitment. It is the volatility, the in-built temporariness of all engagement that counts; it counts more than the engagement itself, which should not outlast the time necessary for consuming the object of desire (or for the desirability of that object to wane).

That all consumption takes time is in fact the bane of a consumer society and a major worry of the merchandisers of consumer goods. Ideally, the consumer's satisfaction ought to be instant, and this in a double sense. Consumed goods should bring satisfaction immediately, requiring no delay, no protracted learning of skills and no lengthy groundwork; but the satisfaction should end the moment the time needed for their consumption is up, and that time ought to be reduced to a bare minimum. This reduction is best achieved if the consumers cannot hold their attention nor focus their desire on any object for long; if they are impatient, impetuous and restive, and above all easily excitable and equally susceptible to losing interest.

When waiting is taken out of wanting and wanting out of waiting, the consumptive capacity of consumers may be stretched far beyond the limits set by any natural or acquired needs or determined by the physical endurability of the objects of desire. The traditional relationship between needs and their satisfaction will then be reversed: the promise and hope of satisfaction will precede the need and will be always greater than the extant need, yet not too great to preclude the desire for the goods which carry that promise. As a matter of fact, the promise is all the more attractive the less the need in question is familiar; there is a lot of fun in living through an experience one did not even know existed and was available. The excitement of the new and unprecedented sensation is the name of the consumer game. As Mark C. Taylor and Esa Saarinen put it, 'desire does not desire satisfaction. To the contrary, desire desires desire';[3] the desire of an *ideal* consumer at any rate. The prospect of the desire fading off, dissipating and having nothing in sight to resurrect it, or the prospect of a world with nothing left in it to be desired, must be the most sinister of the ideal consumer's horrors.

To increase their capacity for consumption, consumers must never be given rest. They need to be constantly exposed to new temptations in order to be kept in a state of a constantly seething, never wilting excitation and, indeed, in a state of suspicion and disaffection. The baits commanding them to shift attention need to confirm such suspicion while offering a way out of disaffection: 'You reckon you've seen it all? You ain't seen nothing yet!'

It is often said that the consumer market seduces its customers. But in order to do so it needs customers who are ready and keen to be seduced (just as, in order to command his labourers, the factory boss needed a crew with the habits of discipline and command-following firmly entrenched). In a properly working consumer society consumers seek actively to be seduced. They live from attraction to attraction, from temptation to temptation, from swallowing one bait to fishing for another, each new attraction, temptation and bait being somewhat different and perhaps stronger than those that preceded them; just as their ancestors, the producers, lived from one turn of the conveyer belt to an identical next.

To act like that is, for the fully-fledged, mature consumer, a compulsion, a must; yet that 'must', that internalized pressure, that impossibility of living one's life in any other way, reveals itself to them in the form of a free exercise of will. The market might have already picked them up and groomed them as consumers, and so deprived them of their freedom to ignore its temptations, but on every successive visit to a market place consumers have every reason to feel in command. They are the judges, the critics and the choosers. They can, after all, refuse their allegiance to any one of the infinite choices on display – except the choice of choosing between them, that is. The roads to self-identity, to a place in society, to life lived in a form recognizable as that of meaningful living, all require daily visits to the market place.

In the industrial phase of modernity one fact was beyond all questioning: that everyone must be a producer first, before being anything else. In 'modernity mark two', the consumers' modernity, the brute unquestionable fact is that one needs to be consumer first, before one can think of becoming anything in particular.

The making of a consumer

In recent years we heard politicians of all political hues speaking in unison, wistfully and enticingly, of 'consumer-led recovery'. Falling output, empty order books and sluggish high-street trade all tend to be blamed on lack of consumer interest or 'consumer confidence' (which means the consumer's desire to buy on credit is strong enough to outweigh their fear of insolvency). The hopes of all these troubles being chased away, of things starting to hum anew, are pinned on the consumers doing their duty again – wishing once more to buy, to buy a lot, and to buy ever more. 'Economic growth', the main modern measure of things being normal and in good order, the main index of a society working as it should, is seen in the consumer society as dependent not so much on the 'productive strength of the nation' (healthy and plentiful labour force, full coffers and daring entrepreneurship of the capital owners and managers), as on the zest and vigour of its consumers. The role once performed by work in linking together individual motives, social integration and systemic reproduction, has now been assigned to consumer activity.

Having dismantled the 'pre-modern' – traditional, ascriptive mechanisms of social placement, which left to men and women only the relatively straightforward task of 'sticking to one's own kind', of living up to (but not above) the standards attached to the 'social category' into which they were born – modernity charged the individual with the task of 'self-construction': building one's own social identity if not fully from scratch, at least from its foundation up. Responsibility of the individual – once confined to obeying the rules that defined in no uncertain terms what it meant to be a nobleman, a tradesman, a mercenary soldier, a craftsman, a farm tenant or a farm hand – now extended to include the choice of social definition itself and having this socially recognized and approved.

Initially, work was offered as the prime tool in coping with this new, modern duty. The sought-after and diligently built social identity took working skills, the site of employment and the career scheme attached to employment as its major determinants. Identity, once selected, had to be built once and for all, for life, and so was in principle at least the employment, the vocation, the life-work. The building of identity was to be steady and consistent, proceeding through a succession of clearly defined stages (no wonder the metaphor of 'building' was picked to convey the nature of 'identity work' to be done), and so was the work-career. The fixed itinerary of work-career and the prerequisites of lifelong identity construction fit each other well.

A steady, durable and continuous, logically coherent and tightly-structured working career is however no longer a widely available option. Only in relatively rare cases can a permanent identity be defined, let alone secured, through the job performed. Permanent, well guarded and assured jobs are now a rarity. The jobs of the old, 'for life', sometimes even hereditary, character are confined to a few old industries and old professions and are rapidly shrinking in number. New vacancies tend to be fixed term, until further notice and part-time. They are often combined with other occupations, and deprived of any safeguards of continuity, let alone of permanence. The catchword is flexibility, and this increasingly fashionable notion stands for a game of hire and fire with very few rules attached, but with power to change the rules unilaterally while the game is still being played.

Nothing truly lasting could be reasonably hoped to be erected on this kind of shifting sand. Purely and simply, the prospect of constructing a lifelong identity on the foundation of work is, for the great majority of people (except, for the time being at least, the practitioners of a few highly skilled and highly privileged professions), dead and buried.

Nevertheless, this momentous departure has not been experienced as a major earthquake or an existential threat. This is because the nature of common preoccupations with identities has also changed in a way which would render the old-fashioned work-careers utterly unsuitable and indeed out of joint with the kind of tasks and worries which the new kind of identity-care entails. In the world in which, according to George Steiner's pithy aphorism, all cultural products are calculated for 'maximal impact and instant obsolescence', a lifelong construction of an a priori designed identity would indeed spell trouble. As Ricardo Petrella put it, the present global trends direct 'economies towards the production of the ephemeral and the volatile – through the massive reduction of the life-span of products and services – and of the precarious (temporary, flexible and part-time jobs)'.[4]

Whatever identity one may contemplate and desire must possess, just like today's labour market, the quality of flexibility. It must be amenable to a change at short notice or without notice and be guided by the principle of keeping all options, or at least as many options as possible, open. The future is bound to be full of surprises, and so proceeding otherwise would amount to a self-deprivation: to the cutting off of the yet unknown, only vaguely intuited benefits that the future meanderings of fate, as well as the unprecedented and unanticipated life-offers, may bring.

Cultural fashions dynamite their entry into the public vanity fair, but they also grow obsolete and turn ludicrously old-fashioned even faster than it takes to grasp public attention. It is therefore better to keep each current identity temporary, to embrace it lightly, to make sure that it will fall away once the arms are open to embrace its new, brighter, or just untested replacement. Perhaps it would be more to the point to speak of self-identity in the plural: the life-itinerary of most individuals is likely to be strewn with discarded and lost identities. Each successive identity is likely to remain incomplete and conditional, and so the snag is how to stave off the danger of its ossification. Perhaps even the very term 'identity' has lost its usefulness, since it belies more than it reveals of the most common life-experience: more and more often concerns with social placement are fed by the fear of an identification too tough and stiff to be revoked if need be. The desire of identity and horror of satisfying that desire, the attraction and the repulsion that the thought of identity evokes, mix and blend to produce a compound of lasting ambivalence and confusion.

Concerns of this kind are much better served by the volatile, infinitely inventive and erratic market of consumer goods. Whether meant for durable or momentary consumption, consumer goods are not, by definition, intended to last forever – no resemblance here to a 'lifelong work career' or 'jobs for life'. Consumer goods are meant to be used up and to disappear; the idea of temporariness and transitoriness is intrinsic to their very denomination as objects of consumption; consumer goods have *memento mori* written all over them, even if with an invisible ink.

And so there is a sort of preordained harmony or resonance between these qualities of consumer goods and the ambivalence endemic to contemporary identity concerns. Identities, just like consumer goods, are to be appropriated and possessed, but only in order to be consumed, and so to disappear again. As in the case of marketed consumer goods, consumption of an identity should not – must not – extinguish the desire for other, new and improved identities, nor preclude the ability to absorb them. This being the requirement there is not much point in looking any further for the tools than the market place. 'Aggregate identities', loosely arranged of the purchasable, not-too-lasting, easily detachable and utterly replaceable tokens currently available in the shops, seem to be exactly what one needs to meet the challenges of contemporary living.

If this is what the energy released by identity problems is expended on, then no specialized social mechanisms of 'normative regulation' or 'pattern maintenance' are necessary; neither do they seem desirable. The traditional, panoptical methods of drill would clearly go against the grain of the consumer's tasks and prove disastrous to the society organized around desire and choice. But would any alternative method of normative regulation fare any better? Is not the very idea of normative regulation, at least on a global-societal scale, a thing of the past? Once crucial to 'get people to work' in a society of working people, did it not outlive its usefulness in the society of consumers? The sole purpose of any norm is to use the human agency of free choice to limit or altogether eliminate freedom of choice; to elbow out or to cut off completely all possibilities except one – the one promoted by the norm. But the side effect of killing choice, and particularly the choice most abominable from the point of view of normative, order-instilling regulation – a volatile, whimsical and easily revokable choice – would be equal to the killing of the consumer in the human being; the most horrifying disaster that may befall the market-centred society.

Normative regulation is thus 'dysfunctional' and so undesirable for the perpetuation, smooth functioning and prosperity of a consumer market, but it also appears repulsive to its clients. The interests of consumers and market operators meet here; in a curious and unanticipated form the message conveyed by the old adage 'what is good for General Motors is good for the United States' comes true (with the proviso, that 'United States' is nothing else but an aggregate of its citizens). The 'consumer spirit', much like the merchandising companies which thrive on it, rebels against regulation. A society of consumers is resentful of all legal restrictions imposed on freedom of choice, of any delegalization of potential objects of consumption, and manifests its resentment by widespread support willingly offered to most 'deregulatory' measures.

Similar resentment is shown in the hitherto unheard-of approval given in the US and elsewhere to the reduction of social services – centrally administered and guaranteed provisions of necessities – providing the reduction goes hand in hand with the lowering of taxes. The slogan of 'more money in the taxpayer's pocket', so popular on the left and right of the political spectrum that it is no longer seriously contested, appeals to consumers' duty to exercise choice, a duty already internalized and reforged into the life-vocation. The promise of more money left in the pocket after taxes is attractive to the electorate not so much for the promise of more consumption, as for the prospect of more choice of what is to be consumed, more pleasures of shopping and choosing; it is to that promise of more frequently exercised choice that it is believed to owe its astonishing seductive power.

For all practical intents and purposes, it is the means, not the end, that counts. Fulfilling the vocation of the consumer means more choosing, whether or not this results in more consumption. To embrace the modality of the consumer means first and foremost falling in love with choice; only in the second, and not at all indispensable place, does it mean consuming more.

Work as judged by aesthetics

Producers can fulfil their vocation only collectively; production is a collective endeavour, it presumes the division of tasks, cooperation of actors and coordination of their activities. Certain partial actions can be performed on occasion singly and in solitude, but even then dovetailing them with other actions which converge on the creation of the final product remains the crucial part of the task and stays high on the performer's mind. Producers are together even when they act apart. The work of each one can only gain from more inter-individual communication, harmony and integration.

Consumers are just the opposite. Consumption is a thoroughly individual, solitary, and in the end lonely activity; an activity which is fulfilled by quenching and arousing, assuaging and whipping up a desire which is always a private, and not easily communicable sensation. There is no such thing as 'collective consumption'. True, consumers may get together in the course of consumption, but even then the actual consumption remains a thoroughly lonely, individually lived-through experience. Getting together only underlies the privacy of the consuming act and enhances its pleasures.

Choosing is more satisfying when performed in the company of other choosers, preferably inside a temple dedicated to the cult of choosing and filled to the brim with worshippers of choice; this is one of the foremost pleasures of going out to dinner in a heavily booked-up restaurant, of milling around a crowded shopping mall or amusement park, of group sex. But what is jointly celebrated in all these and similar cases is the *individuality* of choice and consumption. The individuality of each choice is restated and reconfirmed through being replicated by the copy-cat actions of the crowd of choosers. Were this not so, there would be nothing to be gained by the consumer from consuming in company. The activity of consumption is a natural enemy of all coordination and integration. It is also immune to their influence, rendering all efforts of bonding impotent in overcoming the endemic loneliness of the consuming act. Consumers are alone even when they act together.

Freedom to choose sets the stratification ladder of consumer society and so also the frame in which its members, the consumers, inscribe their life aspirations – a frame that defines the direction of efforts towards self-improvement and encloses the image of a 'good life'. The more freedom of choice one has, and above all the more choice one freely exercises, the higher up one is placed in the social hierarchy, the more public deference and self-esteem one can count on and the closer one comes to the 'good life' ideal. Wealth and income do count, of course; without them, choice is limited or altogether denied. But the role of wealth and income as *capital* – that is, money which serves first and foremost to turn out more money – recedes to a second and inferior place if it does not disappear from view (and from the pool of motivations) altogether. The prime significance of wealth and income is in the stretching of the range of consumer choice.

Hoarding, saving or investing would make sense solely for the promise they hold for the future widening of consumer choice. They are not, however, the options intended for the bulk of ordinary consumers, and were they embraced by a majority of consumers, they would spell disaster. Rising savings and shrinking credit purchases are bad news; the swelling of consumer credit is welcomed as the sure sign of 'things moving in the right direction'. A consumer society would not take lightly a call to delay gratification. A consumer society is a society of credit cards, not savings books. It is a 'now' society. A wanting society, not a waiting society.

Again, there is no need for 'normative regulation' with its attendant disciplining drill and ubiquitous policing to make sure that human wants are harnessed to the market-operators' profits, or any need to reforge the 'needs of economy', the consumer-goods economy, to match the desires of consumers. Seduction, display of untested wonders, promise of sensations yet untried but dwarfing and overshadowing everything tried before, will do nicely. Providing of course, that the message falls on receptive ears and that all eyes are focused on thrill-presaging things when scanning the signals. Consumption, ever more varied and rich consumption, must appear to the consumers as a right to enjoy, not a duty to suffer. The consumers must be guided by aesthetic interests, not ethical norms.

It is aesthetics, not ethics, that is deployed to integrate the society of consumers, keep it on course, and time and again salvage it from crises. If ethics accord supreme value to duty well done, aesthetics put a premium on sublime experience. Fulfilment of duty has its inner, time-extensive logic and so it structures time, gives it a direction, makes sense of such notions as gradual accumulation or delay of fulfilment. The search for experience, however, has no good reason to be postponed, since nothing but 'waste of opportunity' may follow the delay. Opportunity of experience does not need nor justify groundwork, since it comes unannounced and vanishes if not instantly grasped (waning, to be sure, shortly after having been grasped). Opportunity of experience is something to be caught in full flight. There is no peculiar moment especially suitable for doing this. One moment does not differ in this respect from another, each moment is equally good – 'ripe' – for the purpose.

Besides, the choice of the moment is the one choice not available to those who have chosen choice-making as their mode of life. It is not for the consumer to decide when the opportunity of a mind-boggling experience may arise, and so she or he must be ever ready to open the door and welcome it. He or she must be constantly on the alert, permanently capable of appreciating the chance when it comes and doing whatever is needed to make the best of it.

If the producer society is Platonian by heart, seeking unbreakable rules and the ultimate patterns of things, the consumer society is Aristotelian – pragmatic, flexible, abiding by the principle that one worries about crossing the bridge no earlier (but no later either) than one comes to it. The sole initiative left to a sensible consumer is to be on that spot where opportunities are known to be thick on the ground, and be there at the time when they are known to be particularly dense. Such initiative can accommodate only wisdom of a 'phronesis' kind, a collection of rules of thumb, not foolproof recipes and algorithmic commands. Hence it requires a lot of trust, and above all it needs safe havens where that trust can be securely anchored. No wonder a consumer society is also a counselling and advertising paradise, as well as a fertile soil for prophets, fortune-tellers or pedlars of magic potions and distillers of philosophical stones.

To sum up: it is the aesthetics of consumption that now rules where the work ethic once ruled. For the successful alumni of consumer training the world is an immense matrix of possibilities, of intense and ever more intense sensations, of deep and deeper still experiences (in the sense conveyed by the German notion of *Erlebnis*, as distinct from *Erfahrung*; both German terms translate into English as 'experience'. Roughly speaking, *Erlebnis* is 'what I live through', while *Erfahrung* is 'what happens to me'). The world and all its fragments are judged by their capacity to occasion sensations and *Erlebnisse* – the capacity to arouse desire, the most pleasurable phase of the consumer's life pursuits, more satisfying than the satisfaction itself. It is by the varying volumes of that capacity that objects, events and people are plotted on the map; the world map in most frequent use is aesthetic, rather than cognitive or moral.[5]

The status occupied by work, or more precisely by the job performed, could not but be profoundly affected by the present ascendancy of aesthetic criteria. As we have seen before, work has lost its privileged position – that of an axis around which all other effort at self-constitution and identity-building rotate. But work has also ceased to be the focus of particularly intense ethical attention in terms of being a chosen road to moral improvement, repentance and redemption. Like other life activities, work now comes first and foremost under aesthetic scrutiny. Its value is judged by its capacity to generate pleasurable experience. Work devoid of such capacity – that does not offer 'intrinsic satisfaction' – is also work devoid of value. Other criteria (also its supposedly morally ennobling impact) cannot withstand the competition and are not powerful enough to save work from condemnation as useless or even demeaning for the aesthetically-guided collector of sensations.

Vocation as privilege

There is nothing particularly new about jobs differing widely in terms of their capacity to bring satisfaction. Some jobs were always sought-after as being richly satisfying and 'fulfilling', while many others were suffered as drudgery. Certain jobs were 'meaningful' and lent themselves more easily than other kinds of work to being regarded as a vocation, a source of pride and self-esteem. However, the point was that from the ethical perspective no job could be seriously argued to be deprived of value and demeaning; all work added to human dignity and all work equally served the cause of moral propriety and spiritual redemption. From the work ethic point of view, any work – work *as such* – 'humanized', whatever immediate pleasures (or their absence) it held in store for its performers. Ethically speaking, the feeling of a duty fulfilled was the most direct, decisive and in the end sufficient satisfaction work could bring, and in this respect all kinds of work were equal. Even the engrossing, intoxicating sensation of self-fulfilment experienced by the lucky few who could live their trade or profession as a true calling, as a secular mission of sorts, tended to be ascribed to the same awareness of the 'duty well done' which was in principle open to the performers of all jobs, even the meanest and the least engaging. The work ethic conveyed a message of equality; it played down the otherwise obvious differences between jobs, their potentials for satisfaction, their status- and prestige-bestowing capacities, as well as the material benefits they offered.

Not so the aesthetic scrutiny and evaluation of work. This emphasizes distinction, magnifies the differences and elevates certain professions to the rank of engrossing, refined objects of aesthetic, indeed artistic, experience, while denying to other kinds of remunerated livelihood-securing occupations any value at all. The 'elevated' professions call for the same qualities which are demanded for the appreciation of art – good taste, sophistication, discernment, disinterested dedication and a lot of schooling. Other types of work are regarded as so uniformly abject and worthless that by no stretch of the imagination can they become objects of willing, unforced choice. One is likely to perform jobs of that kind only out of necessity and only if one is denied access to any other means of survival.

Jobs in the first category are 'interesting'; jobs in the second category are 'boring'. These two brief verdicts encapsulate complex aesthetic criteria which gives them substance. Their 'no justification needed', 'no appeal allowed' bluntness bear an oblique testimony to the ascendancy of aesthetics now spreading through the land of work, previously a province of ethics. Like everything else which may reasonably hope to become the target of desire and an object of free consumer choice, jobs must be 'interesting' – varied, exciting, allowing for adventure, containing certain (though not excessive) measures of risk, and giving occasion to ever-new sensations. Jobs that are monotonous, repetitive, routine, unadventurous, allowing no initiative and promising no challenge to wits nor a chance for self-testing and self-assertion, are 'boring'. No fully-fledged consumer would conceivably agree to undertake them on her or his own will, unless cast in a situation of no choice (that is, unless his or her identity as a consumer, a free chooser, has already been forfeited, withdrawn or otherwise denied). Such jobs are devoid of aesthetic value and for that reason stand little chance of becoming vocations in a society of experience-collectors.

The point is, though, that in the world where aesthetic criteria rule supreme the jobs in question have not retained their formerly assumed ethical value either. They would be chosen willingly only by people as yet unprocessed by the society of consumers and unconverted to consumerism, and thus satisfied with selling their labour in exchange for bare survival (first generation immigrants and 'guest workers' from poor countries, or the residents of poor countries drawn into factories set by the immigrant capital travelling in search of cheap labour could be said to fall into this category). Others need to be forced into accepting jobs that offer no aesthetic satisfaction. Rough coercion once hidden under the veneer of the work ethic now appears bare-faced and unconcealed. Seduction and arousal of desires, those otherwise unfailingly effective integrating/motivating vehicles of a consumer society, are in this case appallingly irrelevant and toothless. In order to fill jobs that fail the aesthetic test with people already converted to consumerism, a situation of no choice, enforcement and fight for elementary survival must be artificially re-created. This time, though, without the saving grace of moral ennoblement.

Like freedom of choice and mobility, the aesthetic value of work has turned into a potent stratifying factor in the society of consumers. The trick is no longer to limit work time to the bare minimum, so vacating more space for leisure, but on the contrary to efface altogether the line dividing vocation from avocation, job from hobby, work from recreation; to lift work itself to the rank of supreme and most satisfying entertainment. An entertaining job is a highly coveted privilege. And those privileged by it jump headlong into the opportunities of strong sensations and thrilling experience which such jobs offer. 'Workaholics' with no fixed hours of work, preoccupied with the challenges of their jobs twenty-four hours a day and seven days a week, may be found today not among the slaves, but among the elite of the lucky and successful.

Work that is rich in gratifying experience, work as self-fulfilment, work as the meaning of life, work as the core or the axis of everything that counts, as the source of pride, self-esteem, honour and deference or notoriety, in short, work as *vocation*, has become the privilege of the few; a distinctive mark of the elite, a way of life the rest may watch in awe, admire and contemplate at a distance but experience only vicariously through pulp fiction and the virtual reality of televised docu-drama's. That rest is given no chance of living-through their jobs in a way the vocations are lived.

The 'flexible labour market' neither offers nor permits commitment and dedication to any currently performed occupation. Getting attached to the job in hand, falling in love with what the job requires its holder to do, identifying one's place in the world with the work performed or the skills deployed, means becoming a hostage to fate; it is neither very likely nor to be recommended, given the short-lived nature of any employment and the 'until further notice' clause entailed in any contract. For the majority of people other than the chosen few, in the present-day flexible labour market, embracing one's work as a vocation carries enormous risks and is a recipe for psychological and emotional disaster.

Under these circumstances, exhortations to diligence and dedication sound insincere and hollow, and reasonable people would be well advised to perceive them as such – to see through the trappings of apparent vocation into the game their bosses play. Bosses do not really expect employees to believe that they mean what they say – they wish only that both sides *pretend* to believe that the game is for real, and behave accordingly. From the bosses' point of view, inducing the employees to treat the pretence of a vocational pattern to their employment seriously means storing trouble which will erupt whenever the next 'downsizing' exercise or another bout of 'rationalizing' occurs. A short-term success of moralizing sermons would in any case prove counter-productive in the long run, as it would divert people's attention from what ought to be their true vocation – their consumer pursuits.

All this complex intertwining of 'do's' and 'don'ts', of dreams and their costs, of enticements to surrender and warnings against falling into such traps, is offered to the vocation-hungry audience as a spectacle. We see great sportsmen or other stars who reach the peak of their professional skill, but climb to such heights of achievement and fame at the cost of emptying their lives of anything standing in the way of that achievement. They deny themselves all the pleasures that ordinary folk set great store by. Their achievement has all the symptoms of being real. There is hardly a less controversial and more convincing arena in which 'real quality' is tested than the athletics track or the tennis court. And who would doubt the singer's excellence reflected in the riotous delirium of packed theatres? In this public spectacle, there seems to be no room for pretence, confidence tricks, putting on an act, behind-the-scene plots. All this is for real, for everyone to see and pass judgment upon. The drama of vocation is played from the beginning to the end in the open, in front of the faithful crowds. (Or so it seems. The truth, the trustworthiness of the performance, in fact takes a lot of scripting and staging).

The saints of the stardom cult are, like all saints, to be admired and held as an example, but not emulated. They embody, at the same time, the ideal of life and its inachievability. The stars of the stadium and the stage are all inordinately rich. Obviously, their dedication and self-denial bring the fruits that work-lived-as-a-vocation is famed to gestate; recitation of the mind-boggling sums of prizes for the winners of tennis, golf, snooker or chess championships or the footballers' transfer fees are as vital a part of the cult as the recitation of miracles performed or the stories of the martyrdom suffered were in the cult of the saints of faith and piety.

What the saints of the stardom cult surrender in exchange is however as spine-chilling as the gains are awe-inspiring. One of the costs is the transience of their glory. The stars shoot onto the firmament from nowhere and to that nowhere they are bound, and in it they will vanish. No wonder it is the sportsmen and sportswomen who are arguably the best actors of the vocation's morality plays: it is in the nature of their achievement that it must be short-lived, as brief and doomed an episode as youth itself. As displayed by sportswomen and men, work-lived-as-a-vocation is self-destructive, a life towards a speedy end. Vocation may be many things, but what most emphatically it is not – not in this rendition at any rate – is a proposition for the life-project or a whole-life strategy. As displayed by the stars, vocation is, like any other experience in the life of post-modern sensation-gatherers, an *episode*.

Weber's 'Puritan saints' who lived their working lives as deeply ethical endeavours, as fulfilment of divine commandments, could not but see the work of others – any work – as essentially a matter of morality. Today's elite equally naturally tends to view all work as mainly a matter of aesthetic satisfaction. As far as the reality of life at the bottom of the social hierarchy is concerned, this conception, just like the one which preceded it, is a gross travesty.[6] However, it allows one to believe that the voluntary 'flexibility' of the work condition freely and enthusiastically chosen by those at the top, and once chosen cherished and keenly protected, must be an unqualified blessing to everybody else, including those to whom 'flexibility' means not so much freedom of choice, autonomy and the right to self-assert, as lack of security, forced uprooting and an uncertain future.

Being poor in a consumer society

In its halcyon days, in the society of producers, the work ethic reached well beyond the factory floor and the walls of poorhouses. Its precepts informed the vision of a right and proper society yet to be achieved, and until then served as the horizon by which the present moves were oriented and the present state of affairs critically assessed. The vision of the ultimate condition to be reached was that of full employment, of a society consisting solely of working people.

'Full employment' occupied the somewhat ambiguous position of being simultaneously a right and a duty. Depending on which side of the 'labour-hiring contract' the principle was invoked, either one or the other of its two modalities came to the fore; but as with all norms, both aspects had to be present to secure the overall hold of the principle. The idea of full employment as an indispensable feature of 'normal society' implied both a duty universally and willingly accepted and a commonly shared will lifted to the rank of a universal right.

Defining the norm defines also the abnormal. The work ethic encapsulated abnormality in the phenomenon of unemployment – 'abnormal' was not to work. Expectedly, the persistent presence of the poor tended to be explained alternatively by the shortage of work or the shortage of the will to work. The messages of the likes of Charles Booth or Seebohm Rowntree – that one can remain poor while *in* full employment, and therefore the phenomenon of poverty cannot be explained by the insufficient spread of the work ethic – came to the British enlightened opinion as a shock. The very notion of the '*working* poor' had all the markings of a blatant contradiction in terms, certainly as long as the universal acceptance of the work ethic figured most prominently in public thinking about social problems and continued to be seen as the cure-all for social ills.

As work gradually moved away from its central position of the meeting point between individual motives, social integration and systemic reproduction, the work ethic – as we have already noted – was slowly demoted from its function of supreme regulatory principle. By now it had backed out or has been elbowed out from many areas of social and individual life it previously directly or obliquely regimented. The non-working section of the population remained perhaps its last retreat, or rather its last chance of survival. Blaming the misery of the poor on their unwillingness to work, and so charging them with moral depravity and presenting poverty as the penalty for sin, was the last service the work ethic performed in the new society of consumers.

For most of human history the condition of poverty has meant direct jeopardy to physical survival – the threat of death from hunger, medically unattended disease or the lack of shelter. It still means all those dangers in many parts of the globe. Even when the condition of the poor is lifted above the level of sheer survival, poverty always means malnutrition, inadequate protection against vagaries of climate, and homelessness – all defined in relation to what a given society perceives to be the proper standards of nourishment, dress and accommodation.

The phenomenon of poverty does not boil down, however, to material deprivation and bodily distress. Poverty is also a social and psychological condition: as the propriety of human existence is measured by the standards of decent life practised by any given society, inability to abide by such standards is itself a cause of distress, agony and self-mortification. Poverty means being excluded from whatever passes for a 'normal life'. It means being 'not up to the mark'. This results in a fall of self-esteem, feelings of shame or feelings of guilt. Poverty also means being cut off from the chances of whatever passes in a given society for a 'happy life', not taking 'what life has to offer'. This results in resentment and aggravation, which spill out in the form of violent acts, self-deprecation, or both.

In a consumer society, a 'normal life' is the life of consumers, preoccupied with making their choices among the panoply of publicly displayed opportunities for pleasurable sensations and lively experiences. A 'happy life' is defined by catching many opportunities and letting slip but few or none at all, by catching the opportunities most talked about and thus most desired, and catching them no later than others, and preferably before others.

As in all other kinds of society, the poor of a consumer society are people with no access to a normal life, let alone to a happy one. In a consumer society however, having no access to a happy or merely a normal life means to be consumers *manquées*, or flawed consumers. And so the poor of a consumer society are socially defined, and self-defined, first and foremost as blemished, defective, faulty and deficient – in other words, inadequate – consumers.

In a society of consumers, it is above all the inadequacy of the person as a consumer that leads to social degradation and 'internal exile'. It is this inadequacy, this inability to acquit oneself of the consumer's duties, that turns into bitterness at being left behind, disinherited or degraded, shut off or excluded from the social feast to which others gained entry. Overcoming that consumer inadequacy is likely to be seen as the only remedy – the sole exit from a humiliating plight.

As Peter Kelvin and Joanna E. Jarett discovered in their pioneering study of the social-psychological effects of unemployment in a consumer society, one aspect of the situation is particularly painful to people out of work:[7] a 'seemingly unending amount of free time' coupled with their 'inability to make use of it'. 'Much of one's day-to-day existence is unstructured', but the unemployed have no means to structure it in any way recognized as making sense, as satisfying or worthwhile:

> Feeling shut away at home is one of the most frequent complaints of the unemployed . . . unemployed man not only sees himself as bored and frustrated [but] seeing himself like that (as well as actually being so) also makes him irritable. Irritability becomes a regular feature of the day-to-day existence of the unemployed man.'[8]

From his respondents (young male and female unemployed) Stephen Hutchens got the following reports of their feelings about the kind of life they led: 'I was bored, I got depressed easily – most of the time I just sat at home and looked at the paper.' 'I have no money or not enough. I get really bored.' 'I lay in a lot, unless I go to see friends and go to pubs when we have money – not much to boast about.' Hutchens sums up his findings with this conclusion: 'Certainly the most popular word used to describe the experience of being unemployed is "boring" . . . Boredom and problems with time; having "nothing to do" . . .'[9]

Boredom is one complaint the consumer world has no room for and the consumer culture set out to eradicate it. A happy life, as defined by consumer culture, is life insured against boredom, life in which constantly 'something happens', something new, exciting, and exciting because it is new. The consumer market, the consumer culture's faithful companion and indispensable complement, insures against spleen, ennui, over-saturation, melancholy, acidia, being fed up or blasé – all the ailments which once haunted the life of affluence and comfort. The consumer market makes sure that no one at any time may despair or feel disconsolate because of 'having tried it all' and having thus exhausted the pool of pleasures life had to offer.

As Freud pointed out before the onset of the consumer era, there is no such thing as the *state* of happiness; we are happy only for a brief moment when satisfying a vexing need, but immediately afterwards boredom sets in. The object of desire loses its allure once the reason to desire it has disappeared. The consumer market however proved to be more inventive than Freud was imaginative. It conjured up the state of happiness which Freud deemed unattainable. It did this by seeing to it that desires were aroused faster than the time it took to placate them, and that objects of desire were replaced quicker than the time it took to get bored and annoyed with their possession. Not being bored – ever – is the norm of the consumers' life, and a realistic norm, a target within reach, so that those who fail to hit it have only themselves to blame while being an easy target for other people's contempt and condemnation.

To alleviate boredom one needs money – a great deal of money if one wishes to stave off the spectre of boredom once for all, to reach the 'state of happiness'. Desiring comes free, but to desire realistically, and so experience desire as a pleasurable state, requires resources. Medicines against boredom are not available on NHS prescriptions. Money is the entry permit to places where remedies for boredom are pedalled (such as shopping malls, amusement parks or health and fitness centres); the places the presence in which is by itself the most effective of prophylactic potions to ward off the onset of the disease; the places whose principal destination is to keep desires seething, un-quenched and unquenchable, yet deeply pleasurable thanks to anticipated satisfaction.

And so boredom is the psychological corollary of other stratifying factors specific to the consumer society: freedom and amplitude of choice, freedom of mobility, ability to cancel space and structure time. Being the psychological dimension of stratification, it is the one likely to be most painfully felt and most irately objected to by those with low scores. The desperate desire to escape boredom or to mitigate it is also likely to be the main motive for their action.

The odds against their action achieving its objective are, however, enormous. Common remedies against boredom are not accessible to those in poverty, while all unusual, irregular or innovative counter-measures are bound to be classified as illegitimate and bring upon their users the punitive powers of the defenders of law and order. Paradoxically, or not that paradoxically after all, tempting fate by challenging the forces of law and order may itself turn into the poor man's favourite substitute for the affluent consumer's well-tempered anti-boredom adventures, in which the volume of desired and permissible risks are cautiously balanced.

If the constitutive trait of the poor's plight is that of being a defective consumer, there is very little that those in a deprived neighbouhood can do collectively to devise alternative ways of structuring their time, particularly in a fashion recognizable as making sense and being gratifying. The charge of laziness, always hovering dangerously close over the homestead of the unemployed, could be (and was, notably during the Great Depression of the 1930s) fought against with exaggerated, ostentatious and in the end ritualistic busyness around the house – scrubbing floors and windows, washing walls, curtains and children's skirts and trousers, tending to back gardens. There is nothing, though, that one can do to resist the stigma and shame of being an inadequate consumer, even within the ghetto of similarly deficient consumers. Keeping up to the standards of the people around you will not do, since the standards of propriety are set, and constantly raised, far away from the area under the neighbourhood watch, by daily papers and the televised glossy twenty-four-hours-a-day commercials for consumer bliss. None of the substitutes that the local neighbourhood's ingenuity could invent are likely to withstand the competition, warrant self-satisfaction and assuage the pain of glaring inferiority. The assessment of one's own adequacy as a consumer is remotely controlled and the verdict cannot be protested in the court of home-grown opinion.

As Jeremy Seabrook reminds his readers,[10] the secret of present-day society lies in 'the development of an artificially created and subjective sense of insufficiency', since 'nothing could be more menacing' to its foundational principles 'than that the people should declare themselves satisfied with what they have'. What people do have is thus played down, denigrated, dwarfed by obtrusive and all too visible displays of extravagant consumption by the better-off: 'The rich become objects of universal adoration'.

Let us recall that the rich who were put on display as personal heroes for universal adoration used to be 'self-made men', whose lives epitomized the benign effects of the work ethic strictly and doggedly adhered to. This is no longer the case. The object of adoration now is wealth itself – wealth as the warrant for a most fanciful and prodigal lifestyle. It is what one *can* do that matters, not what is to be done or what has been done. Universally adored in the persons of the rich is their wondrous ability to pick and choose the contents of their lives – places to live, partners to live with – and to change these things at will and without effort. They never seem to reach points of no return, there seems to be no visible end to their reincarnations, their future is forever richer in content and more enticing than their past. Last but not least, the only thing that seems to matter to them is the vastness of the prospects which their wealth seems to throw open. These people seem, indeed, to be guided by the aesthetic of consumption; it is their mastery of this aesthetic, not obedience to the work ethic, not their financial success, but their connoisseurship, that lie at the heart of their greatness and their right to universal admiration.

'The poor do not inhabit a separate culture from the rich', Seabrook points out. 'They must live in the same world that has been contrived for the benefit of those with money. And their poverty is aggravated by economic growth, just as it is intensified by recession and non-growth.' It is 'aggravated by economic growth', let us add, in a double sense.

First, whatever is being referred to by the concept of 'economic growth' in its present phase, goes hand in hand with the replacement of jobs by 'flexible labour' and of job security by 'rolling contracts', fixed-term appointments and incidental hire of labour; with downsizing, restructuring and 'rationalizing' – all boiling down to the cutting of the volume of employment. Nothing manifests the connection more spectacularly than the fact that post-Thatcher Britain, the pioneer and the most zealous defender of all such 'factors of growth' and the country widely acclaimed as the most astonishing 'economic success' of the Western world, has been found also the be the site of poverty most abject among the affluent countries of the globe. The latest *Human Development Report* from the UN (United Nations) Development Programme's authorship finds the British poor poorer than those in any other Western or Westernized country. Nearly a quarter of old people in Britain live in poverty, which is five times more than in 'economically troubled' Italy and three times more than in 'falling behind' Ireland. A fifth of British children live in poverty – twice as many as in Taiwan or Italy and six times as many as in Finland. All in all, 'the proportion of poor people in "income poverty" jumped by nearly 60 per cent under [Mrs Thatcher's] government'.[11]

Second, while the poor get poorer, the very rich – those paragons of consumer virtues – get richer still. While the poorest fifth in Britain, the country of the most recent 'economic miracle', are able to buy less than their equivalents in any other major Western country, the wealthiest fifth are among the richest in Europe, enjoying purchasing power equal to that of the legendary rich Japanese elite. The poorer are the poor, the higher and more whimsical are the patterns of life set in front of their eyes to adore, covet and wish to emulate. And so the 'subjective sense of insufficiency' with all the pain of stigma and humiliation which accompany that feeling, is aggravated by a double pressure of decreasing living standards and increasing relative (comparative) deprivation, both reinforced rather than mitigated by economic growth in its present, deregulated, *laissez-faire* form.

The sky which is the limit of consumer dreams rises ever higher while the publicly-managed magnificent flying machines once designed to lift those low down to heaven, first run out of petrol and then are dumped in the scrapyards of 'phased-out' policies or recycled into police cars.

PART TWO

PART TWO

3

The rise and fall of the welfare state

The concept of the 'welfare state' conveys the idea that it is the duty and the obligation of the state to guarantee the 'welfare' (that is, something more than sheer survival: survival with *dignity*, as understood in a given society at a given time) of all its subjects. The concept imposed upon the state-run and state-financed institutions the responsibilities implied by a wider idea of *public welfare*[1] – that of a collective guarantee of individual dignified survival. Public welfare could be seen as a form of collective insurance drawn jointly and extended over every individual member of the collectivity; an insurance policy which promised compensations proportional to the scale of individual need, not to the size of individually-paid premiums. The principle of *public* welfare in its pure form is equality in need, which overrides inequality in the ability to pay. The idea of the welfare state charges state organs with the responsibility for implementing this principle of public welfare.

The idea of public welfare in general and the welfare state in particular has an ambiguous relationship with the work ethic. Indeed, the idea of welfare relates to the core ideas of the work ethic in two opposite ways that are difficult to reconcile, which makes it a topic of a long-standing contention, so far without a resolution acceptable to all sides.

On the one hand, the advocates of a collective guarantee of individual welfare recognized the normality of life supported by work; they pointed out however that the norm is far from being universally upheld because of the lack of permanent employment for all, and that to make the precepts of the work ethic realistic one needs to bail out those who fall by the board. One needs also to see the temporarily unemployed through hard times, keeping them ready to 'behave normally', i.e. to enter employment, once the economy recovers and jobs are again available. By this argument, the welfare state is needed to uphold the power of the work ethic as the norm and the measure of social health, while helping to minimize the adverse effects of the difficulties involved in that norm's constant and universal implementation.

On the other hand, by proclaiming that decent and dignified life should be assured at all times and to all members of the polity 'as a right', *regardless* of their own contribution to common wealth, the idea of public welfare allowed (explicitly or implicitly) for the possibility of separating livelihood from the 'socially useful', productive contributions deemed to be possible solely in employment, and by the same token sapped the work ethic's most sacrosanct and least questioned premise. It rendered the right to dignified life a matter of political citizenship, rather than economic performance.

The contradiction between these two implications is genuine, and so it is little wonder that since its inception at the turn of the century, the welfare state has stood in the centre of controversy. With good reasons, the welfare state was presented by some as the necessary complement of the work ethic, while by others it was viewed as a politically motivated conspiracy against it.

This was not, however, the sole bone of contention. Is the welfare state 'an agency of repression, or a system for enlarging human needs and mitigating the rigours of the free-market economy? An aid to capital accumulation and profits or a social wage to be defended and enlarged like the money in your pay packet? Capitalist fraud or working-class victory?' asked Ian Gough, trying to make sense of the confusion which seemed to be the sole outcome of protracted controversy.[2] The most reasonable answer is that the welfare state has been all these things and many more in addition.

The welfare state emerged at a meeting point between: the pressures of the ailing capitalist economy, incapable of recreating the conditions of its own survival on its own and without political help; the pressures of organized labour, incapable of insuring itself, again on its own and without political help, against the vagaries of 'economic cycles'; the urge to protect and reassert the principle of social inequality through mitigating its most iniquitous and least-endurable manifestations; the desire to stimulate acceptance of inequality by marginalizing those who failed to participate in its reproduction; and the pressing need to help the membership of polity to weather the eroding impact of a politically uncontrolled economy.

Thanks to all these powerful and converging, though heterogeneous drives, the coming of the welfare state at a certain advanced stage of modern (industrial, capitalist, market, democratic) society was indeed 'overdetermined'. The pressures which brought it into being and kept supplying it over the years with renewed vigour were so overwhelming that common wisdom came to see state-administered welfare provisions as a natural ingredient of modern living, much like some form of elected authorities, or some form of currency.

Until quite recently, the enlightened opinion loyally reflected that kind of popular wisdom. Even the most perceptive and insightful of observers found it hard to envisage modern society without a welfare state. In February 1980, in a paper presented in Perugia and published in October 1981, one of the most astute analysts of contemporary trends, Claus Offe, asserted that the welfare state had in a sense 'become an irreversible structure, the abolition of which would require nothing else than the abolition of political democracy and the unions, as well as fundamental changes in the party system'. Offe was in full agreement with the prevailing opinion when he dismissed 'the vision of overcoming the welfare state' as 'not much more than the politically impotent day-dream of some ideologues of the old middle class'. Indeed, the odds against life after the welfare state seemed all but overpowering:

> In the absence of large-scale state-subsidised housing, public education and health services, as well as extensive compulsory social security schemes, the working of an industrial economy would be simply inconceivable . . . The embarassing secret of the welfare state is that, while its impact upon capitalist accumulation may well become destructive . . . its abolition would be plainly disruptive . . . The contradiction is that while capitalism cannot coexist *with*, neither can it exist *without*, the welfare state.[3]

All this rang true, certainly at the time Offe wrote it, and as long as it did, the idea of the abolition or even the serious curtailment of the welfare state, of leaving collective insurance to private initiative and of 'de-etatization' or 'deregulation' of welfare provisions in general, looked to be not much more than a pipe-dream held by ideological fossils. Less than two decades later, though, the unthinkable became thinkable and a state which is not a welfare state and a capitalist economy without the safety net of state-administered securities have become a distinct possibility, if not quite yet the reality in the most affluent and 'economically successful' societies. The pressures to make such a situation a reality appear presently to be overwhelming.

Just what role did the work ethic play or was portrayed as playing in this, by any standards, dramatic reversal of the welfare state's fortune? And what impact may this upheaval have on its future prospects?

Between inclusion and exclusion

It may be difficult for many people today, after the years of 'neo-liberal' mental drill under the political auspices of Margaret Thatcher, Norman Tebbit or Keith Joseph, and the 'neo-liberal' *coup d'état* of Milton Friedman of Friedrich Hayek, to conceive of Sir William Beveridge – if not the father than certainly the midwife of the British welfare state – as a liberal rather than a socialist (if not a leftist critic of social democratic policies). And yet Beveridge saw his blueprint for the comprehensive welfare state as both the legitimate and inevitable fulfilment of the liberal idea of good society: 'I believe that the things I most desire to see done are essentially Liberal things – a carrying forward into the new world of the great living traditions of Liberalism'. Because 'equal enjoyment of all essential liberties' was the 'ultimate aim of Liberalism . . . we can and should use the organised power of the community to increase the rights of individuals'. And the enjoyment of such enhanced liberties and rights will not be equal to all individuals if the community fails to secure, for all of them, 'freedom from Want and fear of Want; freedom from Idleness and fear of Idleness enforced by unemployment . . .'[4]

For a liberal like William Beveridge, it was not enough to declare freedom for all. It was also necessary to see to it that all had the means and the inclination to use that freedom which, according to the law, they had. It was with these preconditions of freedom in mind that Beveridge composed the *Report on Social Insurance and Allied Services* submitted to a government concerned with winning the peace about to follow the war about to be won. That report, in Beveridge's own words:

> sets out a plan for Social Security to ensure that every citizen of the country, on condition of working and contributing while he can, has an income to keep him above want when for any other reason – of sickness, accident, unemployment, or old age – he can not work and earn an income sufficient for the honourable subsistence of himself and all who depend on him, an income sufficient though he has nothing else of his own and not cut down by any means test if he has anything of his own.

It is evident that the report came in the wake of two centuries of the work ethic's unchallenged ascendancy. The work ethic had done its job. It had ground the message home that every sane and able-bodied (male) person would work if he could, and by the middle of the twentieth century this was taken for granted. The sole problem left to be solved was what to do if and when, for whatever reason, work was not available or could not be taken up when it was. It was the fear of such a situation that cut people's wings, paralysed their initiative and deprived them of the courage they needed to face the risks. A communal insurance against such a situation would disperse incapacitating fears and thus give individuals the freedom to take the risks which any effort at self-assertion must entail. Freedom of self-assertion required freedom from want and idleness, and from the fear of either of them.

This idea, understood as primarily a preventive/enabling measure, would not make sense, of course, if such freedoms did not extent to *every* member of the community, not just (after the harm has been done) to those who had already failed – those unlucky or improvident members who 'have nothing else of their own'. To focus help on those who need it most, as most politicians propose today, would not come anywhere near to reaching Beveridge's ambitious objective. Offering assistance only after the fear had already done its devastating job and want and idleness had turned from a frightening eventuality into reality, would do nothing at all to fulfil the liberal dream of daring, self-asserting, self-confident and self-reliant humans.

Even in terms of a purely cost-and-effects calculation, 'focused', means-tested assistance would make a bad business deal. If Beveridge's strategy worked, the welfare state could gradually work itself out of a job; but allowing the fear to haunt people as it did in the past could only multiply the ranks of its victims and so relentlessly push upwards the costs of bailing out those already in need of such assistance. The task therefore was to do away with fear itself, and this could be achieved only if the provisions on offer were 'not cut down by any means test' in the case of the lucky or provident who 'have something of their own'.

It was because of that promise to do away with means tests that Beveridge's vision met with almost universal acclaim. Few, if any people frowned upon the fiscal costs it implied for themselves, while virtually no one complained that 'we cannot afford it' (just like members of an ordinary family accept that everyone has an equal right to food without making first an inventory of the food available and finding out if there is enough to quell everybody's appetite). As Alan Deacon and Jonathan Bradshaw point out in their excellent history of the means test[5], it was indeed to the promise to abolish the means test that the Beveridge Report owed its 'tremendous popularity'.

When the National Insurance Bill finally became law, *The Economist* (2 February 1946) interpreted it as the 'virtual abolition of the means test'. As a matter of fact, the abolition never really happened: by the end of 1948 there were in Britain three means-tested benefits, used by around two million people. This number has however been dwarfed into insignificance by the unstoppable rise in the number of means-tested social services in later years. By December 1982 some form of means test already affected twelve million people – a pace of growth hardly matched in any other field of public life.

Universal and selective (means tested) provisions of social benefits create two entirely different models of the welfare state; different in their social and cultural impact, in the way they are perceived by various categories of population, and in the prospects of their political fortunes.

No one perhaps fought more passionately against the gradual yet relentless replacement of universalist ambitions with selective practices than Richard Titmuss and Peter Townsend. In his desperate attempt to stem the rising tide, Titmuss reminded his readers in 1968[6] that 'services for the poor were always poor services' – when confined to the poor part of the population notorious for its lack of political muscle and public audibility, selective social provisions tend to attract on the whole the worst, rather than the best, professionals and managers. Both authors repeatedly argued, however, that whether this already very serious handicap was or was not real, confinement of social provisions to the means-tested poor had yet farther-reaching deleterious consequences for the community as a whole. Only when social services are aimed at the community as a whole and so are seen as benefiting everybody, could they 'foster social integration and a sense of community as they had done during the war'.[7]

Indeed, abolition of the means test invites the community of beneficiaries (overlapping in such cases with the totality of the population) to view the welfare state's expenditures as money well spent; the money spent was used, after all, to cover the cost of the best, most generous and most trustworthy insurance against all sorts of bad luck which 'one can buy'. The community itself is then seen as a secure home and the site where the proper (and optimal) balance of rights and duties is day-by-day drawn. Confine the provision of services to a means test and the community is immediately split into those who give without getting anything in exchange, and those who get without giving (a perception well illustrated recently by David Blunkett, a minister of the newly-elected 'New Labour' government, who in a letter to the *Guardian* of 29 July 1997 reduced the welfare state idea – which he proclaimed 'innefective and unsustainable' – to 'passing cash from one section of the community to another'). Rationality of interest is thereby set against the ethics of solidarity and the ethics themselves become a matter of what one 'can afford', or rather what one politically wills to share.

The overall effect of means testing is division instead of integration; exclusion instead of inclusion. The new, smaller community of taxpayers constitutes itself by using its political muscle to constitute the category of deficient citizens, and then pulling its own ranks together in a determined effort to marginalize that category and punish it for failing to live up to the standards advertised as the trademark of the constituting and self-constituting core. The indignant and self-righteous verdict, like that of R. Boyson[8], that money is taken 'from the energetic, successful and thrifty to give to the idle, the failures and the feckless', finds then a growing number of sympathetic ears. The receivers of what now bears an uncanny resemblance to extorted pay-outs *must be* feckless, so that the majority, can ascribe its own good fortune to thriftiness, and they *must be* failures, so that the majority can treat its own kind of life as a success story. As Joel F. Handler remarked, through the stigmatization of the outcasts the genuine or putative values of the dominant part of society are reaffirmed: 'observers construct themselves by constructing others'.[9]

The inventory of damages does not end here. Arguably the most seminal long-term effect of the kind of welfare state which has been reduced to servicing the needs of a small and, in popular opinion, inferior section of the population, is the impoverishment of politics and fading of political interest among the citizenship at large. For the majority of citizens, interest in the polity boils down to keeping the hands of the exchequer away from their pockets. There are virtually no other stakes – there is little else they would expect the state to offer, and so they see less and less reason to engage actively in the political life of the community. The 'downsizing' of the welfare state goes hand in hand with the wilting and shrinking of the politically active citizenship.

The welfare state unemployed

Such seem to be the 'unanticipated consequences' (or, as Zsuzsa Ferge and S.M. Miller would suggest[10], the 'quasi-intentional', 'directed but unplanned' outcomes) of the relentless drift towards means testing. One wonders, though, whether deleting the generation of 'community feeling' from the list of the welfare state's tasks was indeed – as it has been alternatively suggested by Titmuss and Townsend on the one hand and the advocates of 'focused assistance' on the other – just a matter of fatal short-sightedness or an unwanted, but unavoidable outcome of worsening economic balances.

As it has been indicated before, the explosive entry of the welfare state into the industrialized part of the world, its initially astounding political success and the virtual absence of serious resistance to its progress, were all due to its 'over-determination': to the convergence of many interests and pressures coming from otherwise antagonistic corners. Keeping the provisions of the welfare state intact used to be ascribed time and again to an unwritten 'social contract' between the social classes who without it would be at each other's throats. The amazing persistence of the welfare state used to be explained by its peace-making and peace-keeping function: it better protected the acceptance by the workers of the rules set by their capitalist bosses, and did this at a lower cost than the work ethic, supported solely by coercive measures, would ever have been able to do.

Conversely, the present-day implosion of the welfare state, the fast evaporation of support in quarters once eager to make it work, and the equanimity with which the curtailment and withdrawal of its provision and even the abandonment of its ostensibly unshakeable principles are viewed, all suggest a similar 'over-determination'. To explain the reversal of the welfare state's fortunes by an ideological change of guard and the inroads made into the public mood by neo-liberal, monetarist or neo-conservative propaganda, would be equal to putting the cart before the horse. The question that needs to be answered first is why the neo-liberal propaganda found such a wide and grateful audience and seemed to hit the target almost hands down. Claus Offe got it right when he wrote in 1987, in an article under the pertinent title 'Democracy Against the Welfare State?', that the fact that the welfare state is rapidly losing its political support 'cannot be fully explained either by economic and fiscal crisis arguments, or by political arguments emphasizing the rise of neoconservative elites and ideologies; nor can it be undone by moral appeals to the justice and legitimacy of existing welfare state arrangements'.[11]

Indeed, all such common arguments are in the end political rationalizations and ideological justifications of the measures taken, rather than their explanation. The rise of neo-conservative elites is not an explanation, but itself a phenomenon to be explained. Another mystery which needs explanation is why the 'moral appeals to justice and legitimacy', which once prompted and boosted the welfare state's steady expansion, are now deployed almost without exception in the service of its radical reduction and disbanding.

With all its over-determination, the initial political popularity of the welfare state would be inconceivable inside a capital-dominated society if not for the resonance between welfare-state style public insurance and the needs of a capitalist economy. Among its many other functions, the welfare state performed a crucially important role in the perpetual 'recommodification of labour'; by providing good quality education, an adequate health service, decent housing and healthy nourishment for the children of poor families, it assured a steady supply of the capitalist industry with employable labour – an effect no individual company or group of companies would be able to secure on their own. As the perpetuation of the capitalist mode of production depends on the constant purchase of labour, prospective labour must be made into a commodity which the prospective employers would be willing to buy; the employers could not and would not purchase an inferior product. The welfare state kept a 'reserve army' of labour in a state of constant readiness for active service, and kept it in the right shape and condition while its services were not needed.

However, the prospect of employers needing again the services of the reserve army of labour presently under state-administered care are growing increasingly remote. Presently redundant labour may never again become a commodity – not so much because of its own defective quality, as due to the absence of demand. Such a demand as is still likely to emerge on the domestic labour market – demand for casual, occasional and 'flexible' (that is, not 'exceedingly profiled' or 'overtrained') labourers, is likely to ignore the kind of well educated, robust and self-confident labour force that the welfare state in its halcyon days sought to cultivate. Even those relatively small quantities of old-style labour that parts of modern industry may still need are likely to be sought and found far beyond the reach of any single state, given the finances' new unbound freedom of movement and the much cherished flexibility of deregulated capitalist enterprise. A recent commentary by Martin Woollacott grasps this trend well:

> The Swedish-Swiss conglomerate Asea Brown Boveri announced it would be cutting its West European work force by 57,000, while creating other jobs in Asia. Electrolux followed with the announcement that it will cut its global work force by 11 per cent, with most of the cuts in Europe and North America. Pilkington Glass also announced significant cuts. In just ten days, three European firms had cut jobs on a scale large enough to be compared with the numbers mentioned in the new French and British governments' proposals on job creation . . . Germany, notoriously, has lost 1 million jobs in five years, and its companies are busy building plants in Eastern Europe, Asia, and Latin America. If West European industry is massively re-locating outside Western Europe, then all these arguments about the best government approach to unemployment would have to be seen as of limited relevance.[12]

Employers were glad to shift the cost of the 'recommodification of labour' to the Treasury as long as the fate of profitable production hung on the labour force being increased. This has gradually ceased to be the case, however. Most of the gains in company results have been attained through 'up-front' expenditures (reaching around 80 per cent of total costs) which do not include the engagement of more labour. More and more, the hiring of labour is turning from an asset into a liability. Managers, particularly the top managers of top companies, are richly rewarded for the successful 'downsizing' of their staff – for example, Thomas Labrecque, the director-general of Chase Manhattan Bank, who was voted a salary of nine million dollars in recognition of his role in eliminating 10,000 jobs. The priorities of shareholders are shared and reinforced by the Stock Exchange. Louis Schweitzer, the boss of Renault, was justly baffled and aggrieved by the angry reaction of public opinion to the closure of Renault plants in Belgium; the move had, after all, the unqualified backing of the Stock Exchange – the ultimate expression of business wisdom – which reacted to it by adding 12 per cent to the value of Renault shares.[13]

However cumbersome tax-wise, the state-administered welfare services were from the companies' point of view good investments, assuming that an additional labour force would need to be hired if a company wished to expand, and that it was from the pool of the state-welfare users that companies would need to draw whenever they wished to replenish their labour resources. Given however the present-day tendency to measure the effects of business by the share-and-dividends value rather than the volume of product, as well as the rapidly falling role of labour in production and the global dimensions of companies' freedom, the investment in welfare provision does not seem all that profitable after all; the same and better effects may be obtained at much less cost. The 'flags of convenience' cheaply obtained in the far-away places under the aegis of less demand-burdened governments seem to be a much better idea. What they promise is opportunity without responsibility, and when such 'making economic sense' opportunities come by, few sound-minded businessmen, hard pressed by the stern demands of competitiveness, would insist on their responsibilities.

This newly-obtained freedom of movement comes together with freedom from the financial burden of replenishing the pool of labour: seemingly inexhaustible reservoirs of raw, pliable and unspoiled labour beckon and lure from afar. On a planet covered in part by societies of sophisticated consumers, there are still vast virgin territories where submissiveness of labour may be obtained without the need to whip up consumer desires; where the rough demands of the struggle for survival will do the job which elsewhere calls for inventing ever-new desires clamouring for satisfaction and for keeping wages up so that these desires can turn into universal needs.

This seems to be the logic of capitalist reproduction: having manoeuvred itself into the use of consumer desires as the major mobilizing and integrating force and the royal road to conflict-resolution and order-maintenance, the capitalist approach tends in the long run to 'price labour out of work'. Each successive plot ploughed up by the capitalist mode of production suffers sooner or later from soil exhaustion and falls victim to the law of diminishing returns. In order to keep production profitable, new – virgin, uncultivated – lands must be sought. This predicament goes a long way towards explaining the pressure to dismantle all the barriers to free trade and above all to the free movement of capital. All the more so, as that pressure goes hand in hand with another pressure to make the walls barring free movement of labour watertight. What is happening now on a global scale is the Mohammeds of capital finding travel to the mountains of labour much more convenient and less expensive than calling the mountains to join them at home.

And so the 'reserve army of labour' and the costs of its readiness for active service are now global, while all welfare provisions are state-bound and – like the state authority itself – local. The arms of the state are much too short to reach where it truly counts. To the expansion and security of capital the old-style state's assistance has become largely irrelevant. The local businessmen knowing only too well that to remain businessmen they better stop being local, need their prime-ministers and foreign secretaries mostly as their trade agents to introduce and endear them to the authorities of the targeted localities during their diplomatic voyages, and if need be to subsidize the trips.

And so the paramount interest, arguably the main axis in the cluster of interests which stood at the cradle of the welfare state, has been removed from the project it once held together. Without it, the whole cluster falls apart, losing, above all, its economic foundation. Seeing no benefit in paying for the 'recommodification' of labour which they are unlikely ever again to need, businessmen worth their salt use their new global freedoms to take their money and their enterprise abroad, to less demanding places, the moment they are asked to partake of the costs of welfare. The governments who insist on keeping the standards of welfare intact are therefore haunted by the fear of a 'double whammy': the homeless and disinherited flocking in, the capital (and so the potential income sources) flocking out.

Conceivably, employers could be persuaded to stay only if allowed to push down the costs of local labour; but in this the state guarantee of minimum survival, that hard core of the welfare-state idea, is a major obstacle, rather than a help. Besides, and perhaps more importantly yet, the successful pauperization of the local labour force on a massive scale would in the long run, or perhaps quicker than that, prove counter-productive. Local employees are also the local consumers, and it is in their solvency and willingness to pay that the producers of consumer goods vest their hope of economic success and seek their insurance against falling profits and bankruptcies.

Despite being threatened by the crumbling of its economic foundation, cannot the welfare state still be kept on course by the cross-party and cross-class political support it once enjoyed? After all, history kept showing us until recently that the more inclusive democracy becomes, the more decisively it presses towards the defence of the weak and the collective insurance against weakness. The right to vote, from the moment it became universal, was used over and over again to bring into power the politicians who promised to do just that – to repair collectively the blights and pains suffered individually. The principle of the welfare state seemed safe in democracy's hands. Indeed, the unstoppable growth of the state-administered protection of the weak inspired political scientists from T.H. Marshall on to include social rights into the very notion of democratic citizenship; to see such rights as the inevitable product of democracy's logic.

Popular theories explained that logic by suggesting, somewhat romantically, that democratic practices as such cultivate a feeling of shared responsibility for the well-being of the community as a whole. Some analysts added that since no one – including the currently better-off – among the members of the political community can be truly safe in her or his status as a citizen without a reliable safety net, insuring against a fall beneath the standards required for a dignified life, some form of collective protection, was indispensable also to those who at the moment could stand on their own feet. In other words, for almost a century the visible logic of democratic politics led observers to assume that although some people need more social services than others and need them more urgently than the others do, the existence of such services and their universal availability is in the 'well understood' interest of all.

The contented majority?

For two decades now the facts of political life seem to deny the above deductions. In one country after another the majority of voters give their support to parties that explicitly demand the curtailment of welfare provisions, or promise more benign taxation of individual incomes which would inevitably have the same effect. 'Raising taxes' has become an anathema on politicians' lips and an abomination to electors' ears.

The astounding unanimity on this point among the parties across the political spectrum served some analysts as a main argument to assert the advent of a new 'solidarity' of sorts; of a new political consensus 'beyond left and right'. What is glossed over in such an assertion, though, is the fact that not that long ago the support for the welfare state was also a virtually non-party issue, 'beyond left and right', and a basis and expression of genuine cross-class solidarity. The attitude to welfare-state policies has traditionally commanded wide democratic consensus. It still commands consensus today, just as it did half a century ago, only the attitude which commands consensus today is the very opposite of that which enjoyed almost universal support then. It is this change of axis around which the democratic consensus is built that needs explaining.

No one explained better this amazing sea-change in public mood and its political effects – still unpredictable a mere two decades ago even for the most perceptive of scholars – than John Kenneth Galbraith in his discussion of the 'contented majority'. How can it be, asks Galbraith, that the majority of voters in a democratic polity give freely their support to the increase of social inequality? It never happened before, not since voting rights became truly democratic, not since they had been extended from the propertied classes to all adults and made universal.

There must have been a good reason for this being the case. After all, the poor and indolent, people who could not eke out a passable life and make ends meet on their own, were always a minority – even a politically insignificant minority. Besides, they were the least likely to register their vote at the polling booths; neglecting their interests and wishes was always comparatively easy and in no way jeopardized the chances of a politician. That majority which favoured some redistribution of wealth, the levelling up of inequalities and above all the collective guarantees of individual well-being, must have therefore come from different quarters. They most certainly included the 'median voter', placed comfortably at a secure distance from the extremes of poverty. Those who voted in favour of the state-serviced safety net must have been people who did not necessarily intend to use that net right away; even such people who earnestly hoped never to need to use it at all. On the face of it, they must have acted altruistically: ready to make a personal sacrifice unlikely to be rewarded in a foreseeable future, and optimally not to be rewarded at any time. What made them to behave like this?

In all probability, the genuine reason to act in this way was their lack of self-confidence. They might have managed on their own *so far*, but how could they know that their luck – since this *was* a matter of luck – would last forever? The world around them was notorious for making any prosperity uneven, patchy and shaky. This was a world that saw the most spectacular of fortunes vanish without trace, drawing into abyss myriads of lesser, more vulnerable existences. Just how resourceful did one need to be, to be really sure of one's security? Is it not rather the case that security requires foundations more powerful and reliable than anything which the most diligent of individual efforts may conjure up? Under the circumstances, this seemed to be a fairly reasonable question to ask; and a rhetorical question at that, inviting one and only one answer.

Circumstances must have changed, though, since the question is now seldom asked and, if asked, suggests an entirely different answer. Most middle-range voters seem to be pretty sure that they will be better off when managing their affairs on their own. They still need an insurance against bad luck and other contingencies, since they control them no better than their fathers did, but they reckon that the kind of insurance they can afford to buy privately will offer them more and better benefits than the degraded, averaged-down services of the state are likely to provide. To put it in a nutshell, the new mood is not so much a question of self-confidence, but merely a sober reflection on the fact that all alternatives to self-reliance now seem even less prepossessing than the risks the self-reliance inevitably entails.

This new conviction (or new resignation to the inevitable) changes the balance between the sacrifices made to keep welfare provisions available and the value of such provisions; or, at least, it modifies the way in which that balance is weighed in tranquil and happy moments, when resorting to state assistance seems an utterly improbable emergency. Money left in one's own pocket thanks to the lowering of taxes seems a much better prospect than the largely abstract possibility of public care, whose standards, and attractiveness, are falling, in any case, by the day. Public provision, to put it simply and in a form readily understandable nowadays, is *not* 'good value for money'.

The way in which the median voter views the balance between fiscal costs and welfare benefits has changed for two further reasons as well (which, to be sure, obliquely reinforce the feeling of confidence and the desire of self-reliance simply by rendering the alternative ever less appetizing).

The first reason is the long-term effects of the principle of means-testing. One of these effects is the steady and relentless deterioration of the quality of welfare services. In line with expectations, once they are reserved for those who need them these services cannot count on the political muscle of those others who (at least thus far) 'need them not', and so become a natural target for economies sought by politicians in order to lower taxes, and thus to curry the favours of those more fortunate others. People in need, on the other hand, are notorious for lacking any political muscle of their own.

Quite recently the newly-elected socialist government of France, making the meeting of the budgetary criteria for admission to the single currency its priority, entered the long-avoided road of means testing by introducing an income ceiling for the heretofore universal family allowances. On this occasion, summing up the experience of all the other countries who started earlier on the same route, Serge Halimi observed:

> One starts from denying to the middle classes equal access to certain collective provisions. Then these provisions appear more and more associated with the disprivileged – who alone benefit from them. Sums devoted to the provisions shrink unstoppably, according to the rule that, in an American expression, 'programmes for the poor are poor programmes'. Sooner or later, discoveries are made of 'fraud, deception and abuse': a single mother, ususally a black one, who uses her food coupons to buy vodka (a constant refrain in Reaganite discourse), the irresponsible poor, who bear children encouraged by the welfare provisions etc. The last stage; the popularity of welfare protection having evaporated, the middle classes, no more interested in its continuation, agree to its abolition.[14]

To confine the benefits of the welfare state to the politically-marginalized section of the potential electorate is a faultless recipe for reducing the quality of benefits to a level which, in the eyes of the slightly less impoverished sections of the population, will make even the most dubious of provisions offered by private insurers look sheer luxury by comparison. (It would be interesting, though, to measure the extent to which the deterioration of

state-managed insurance lowered also the quality of private insurance provisions, and so lowered the general level of expectations.) The poor (and
increasingly poor) quality of welfare benefits is the best argument against
the expenditure they require: their value is getting so low that to the majority of the electorate any money spent for their purpose seems wasted.

Another effect of protracted means testing is the stigma attached to the
recipients of welfare. The message hammered home, even if not spelled out
in so many words, is that needing assistance is a sign of failure to live up to
the standards which most other people seem to manage quite well to meet.
Applying for benefit is therefore an admission of failure. A shameful, self-
excluding, self-marginalizing decision, in view of the fact that most people
never seem to reach into the public purse (whatever they get in the form of
tax relief, professional privileges and perks, or overt and oblique business
subsidies, is in the public vocabulary to their credit, not their debit). Applying for benefit is a most unattractive prospect, which makes all alternatives,
whatever their quality, look more reasonable and desirable.

The second reason is the advent of the consumer society and the entrenchment of consumerist culture. Consumerism puts the highest premium on
choice: choosing, that purely formal modality, is a value in its own right,
perhaps the sole value of consumerist culture which does not call for, nor
allow, justification. Choice is the consumer society's meta-value, the value
with which to evaluate and rank all other values. And no wonder, since the
'choosiness' of the consumer is but a reflection of competitiveness, the lifeblood of the market. To survive, and even more to thrive, the consumer
market must first shape the consumer in its own image: the choice is what
competition offers, and discrimination is what makes the offer attractive.

The myth of a discriminating consumer and the myth of the market as
the purveyor of free choice and the guardian of freely-asserted preferences
nourish and cultivate each other. Without the first, the second would be
hardly imaginable. The right type of consumer is a person who cherishes
the right to choose more than the object of choice, and celebrates visits to
the market place as the public manifestation of connoisseurship. The wide
assortment of goods on display, and the possibility of selecting one object
rather than another, lifts even an unrefined dilettante to the rank of a con-
noisseur, while being a skillful, cultivated chooser is, in a consumer society
– a society stratified according to the ability to choose – a most coveted
accolade. The conviction of being a cultivated practitioner of choice is
richly gratifying.[15]

The no-choice situation – taking what one is given solely because nothing else is on offer; having no voice in the selection – is, accordingly, the
anti-value of the consumer society. Being deprived of choice is in itself
degrading and humiliating, whatever its effects on the well-being of the
deprived; it is also a deeply dissatisfying, joyless and annoying condition.
Goods acquire their lustre and attractiveness in the course of being chosen;
take the choice away, and their allure vanishes without trace. An object
'freely chosen' has the power to bestow that distinction on its chooser

which objects 'just allotted' obviously do not possess. The fully-fledged consumer will therefore put choice, with all the risks and the unfamiliar, often frightening traps involved, above the relative security carried by rationing and allotment.[16] The ideal type of consumer will tolerate a great deal of relative inferiority of the object of consumption just because it has been 'freely chosen' and not assigned.

For this reason the institution of the welfare state is starkly out of tune with the climate of a consumer society, whatever the quality of its provisions are. If the marketing of products cannot operate without promoting (through lip service at least) the cult of *difference* and choice, the idea of the welfare state makes little sense without appealing to the idea of the *sameness* of the human condition, human needs and human rights. Consumerism and the welfare state are therefore at cross-purposes. The odds are against the welfare state; the pressure of consumer mentality is overwhelming. Even if the state-offered services were of much better quality than they are, they would still be burdened with the fundamental flaw of being exempt from allegedly free consumer choice – a flaw that discredits them beyond redemption in the eyes of converted and devoted, 'born again' consumers.

Success that brought the demise

All this having been said, the question remains: how come so many denizens of modern society turned into sophisticated consumers? How come that a significant majority now prefer to make their own consumer choices rather than the less risky reliance on the guaranteed provision of all basic necessities? How come that a significant majority are now content with being left to their own resources, counting on nothing but their own wit and ingenuity? Perhaps the following example will offer some insight into the reasons.

For the last decade or so, a wave of protest against so-called 'affirmative action' (the positive discrimination in employment, promotion and college admission in favour of black and Hispanic candidates coming from admittedly deprived social strata and standing therefore little chance in an open competition against the socially better situated and 'cultured' whites) swept America, aided and abetted by the conservative appointees of the Reagan-Bush era to the Supreme and Federal Courts. The protest was something to be expected, as many white parents were nonplussed and angry at nominally inferior students taking up the university places which their own sons and daughters missed despite achieving better test scores. What did come as a surprise, however, was a considerable and growing number of Afro-Americans among the protesters. In fact, the first Democrat who won a place in the State legislature on the 'abolition platform', demanding an end to 'affirmative action', was Ward Connerly, a wealthy black Californian businessman. Decried and vilified by many black and Hispanic activists,

Connerly nevertheless enjoyed significant overt or tacit support among the expanding ranks of the increasingly affluent Afro-American middle class. The argument which strikes a particularly sensitive chord among the latter is one of dignity of self-assertion. The presence of 'affirmative action' belittles and devalues the success of those numerous blacks who 'did it' and 'have arrived'. It would certainly be more gratifying if no one had reason to think that their achievement was undeserved – a gift rather than the product of conscious effort, personal talent, diligent work and the right choice of lifestyle.

Supporters of Connerly are, in effect, saying, 'we do not need crutches', 'we can move very well on our own legs'. But from where did this sudden self-confidence come? The answer slipped from Connerly's tongue: 'everybody can make it, because the playing field is a lot closer to level now'.[17] But the playing field has been levelled thanks to 'affirmative action', and this is that action's undeniable success and historic accomplishment. One in three black families has now an annual income at or above the American average (currently $35,000); it was less than one in four a mere 25 years ago. More than one in five black families now boasts an income above $50,000 – in America, the index of affluence. There are thousands and thousands of black lawyers, doctors, company managers – people who are heard and who can make themselves be heard. Would all this have happened without 'affirmative action'? According to research recently completed by the New York University Law School, of 3435 blacks who became law students and so got a chance of joining one of America's most lucrative professions, only 687 would have achieved entry to the school just on the strength of their test results.

One can say that, in less than a quarter of a century, 'affirmative action' has achieved an objective similar to that which moved the founding fathers of the welfare state: it has 'worked itself out of a job'. But if that has indeed happened, it certainly did not happen in the way the visionaries imagined. Thanks to the positive discrimination, a new, self-confident, black middle class has been born. Its members do not want to be reminded that they are where they are not because they exercised their own wit and industry, like other Americans do or are supposed to be doing, but because they have been helped there by loading the chances. It is an integral part of their bid for dignity to proclaim loud and clear that if they have 'done it' then everyone else can too, and if some cannot, it must be because they are not trying hard enough. This would imply, after all, that they who did it, did it thanks to trying as they should have.

For this to sound credible, their poorer and less resourceful fellows-in-fate must be looked upon with suspicion and disdain; above all, one needs to demand the dismantling of 'privileges', that vexing reminder of one's own 'impaired' (because assisted) progress. Those who have reached the top no longer need the state-provided ladder and are eager to send it to the scrap yard. Those who climbed it first are the first to declare it useless and to complain of the iniquitous, degrading shadow it casts on the users.

This is not, however, the meaning which 'working itself out of a job' had for the inventors of the welfare state or 'affirmative action'. What they had in mind was getting rid of that deprivation which made collective care or positive discrimination necessary in the first place: to compensate for the inequality of chances and thus make chances equal. What did in fact happen is something quite different: people whom the community helped to rise above their initially inferior position not only lost the need for assistance, but turned into its keenest detractors. In a sense, 'affirmative action' bred its own gravediggers. After all, the black affluent professionals, who rose to the ranks of the upper-middle class straight from the ghetto, have more reason than their new white companions to feel righteous about censuring the 'nanny state' and more chance to sound, while doing so, sincere and believable: they have arrived, they have done it, they have proved that it can be done, so let others do the same. But can those others do the same now that the 'degrading' adjustment of scores in relation to skin colour is no longer available? At the University of Texas Law School, there were 5.9 per cent of black freshers last year. This year, with positive discrimination declared illegal, the proportion will be 0.7 per cent. Who will carry the indignation of Ward Connerly into the next generation?

The cases of 'affirmative action' and the welfare state are not of course identical (the idea of the welfare state in its original form militated against any discrimination, while the discrimination it promoted in its later stages was anything but 'positive') but the socio-psychological mechanism of 'working itself out of a job' operates in both cases in quite similar a fashion. Galbraith's 'contented majority' is in no small measure a *product* of the welfare state, and the sediment of its success.

The welfare state came nowhere near the fulfilment of its founding fathers' dreams of exterminating once for all poverty, humiliation and despondency; yet it did produce a large enough generation of well educated, healthy, self-assured, self-reliant, self-confident people, jealous of their freshly acquired independence, to cut the ground from beneath the popular support for the idea that it is the duty of those who have succeeded to assist those who continue to fail. It is to the ears of this generation, empowered by the welfare state, the 'self-made' men and women who would not be self-made if not for the material assistance or reassuring impact of a ready-to-help community, that the arguments about the disempowering impact of collective insurance and social wages are most telling. It is far from clear, though, whether the truth of such arguments will outlive the generation most inclined to accept them as true.

There are good reasons to suppose, as Martin Woollacott recently put it, that what the authors of the present turn-around like to present as the solution to the real or imputed contradictions of the welfare state boils down in fact to:

merely taking advantage of what, historically, is just a moment – that moment when the social capital created by the welfare state has not been yet wholly dissipated and the new social costs caused by the decline of the welfare state have not yet been huge. The social costs of both the welfare state and the non-welfare state are large, but the social costs of a state in transition between the two can be ignorantly or mendaciously represented as small. Small they may be, but only for a time.[18]

---------(**4**)

The work ethic and
the new poor

◯────────────────────────────────

The early nineteenth-century preachers of the work ethic knew full well what they were talking about. At that time labour was the sole source of wealth; to produce more, and to involve more labour in the process of production, meant much the same thing. There were growing ranks of entrepreneurs eager to produce more, and there were growing ranks of paupers reluctant to work and produce on the entrepreneurs' terms. The work ethic could, conceivably, induce the two to meet. The idea of work as the road leading simultaneously towards a wealthy nation and out of individual poverty rang true.

In the late twentieth century, the work ethic comes once more to the forefront of public debate; it looms large in both the diagnoses of current ills and the prescriptions for their cure. It is most prominent in the welfare-to-work programmes, initiated in the USA but, since their inception (though regardless their dubious results), enviously eyed by a growing number of politicians in other affluent countries (including Britain). As Handler and Hasenfeld point out about WIN (the cryptonim for the American welfare-to-work programme):

> from its inception and throughout its convoluted history, the rhetorics justifying WIN bore little relationship to its actual impact. All the available evidence indicates that the programme has had dismal results . . . Work policies and programmes have persisted in various forms, despite the overwhelming historical evidence that they have generally failed to reduce the welfare rolls in any appreciable way or to improve the economic self-sufficiency of the poor. The reasons for their survival cannot, therefore, reside in their salutary effects on the poor and welfare, but rather in their apparent utility to the nonpoor.[1]

The reluctance, genuine or putative, of the present-day welfare poor to join in the productive effort in no way arrests the growth of productivity.

The present-day corporations do not need more workers to increase their profits, and if they *do* need more workers they can easily find them else-where and on better terms than those attainable locally, even if this leads to the further impoverishment of the local poor. After all, according to the latest *Human Development Report* from the UN, 1.3 billion of the world population live currently on a dollar a day or less; by these standards, even the 100 million people living below the poverty line in the affluent West, the homeland of the work ethic, have a long way to go.

But in the world of big corporations progress means today first and foremost 'downsizing', while technological progress means replacement of living labour with electronic software. Just how duplicitous the condemnation of welfare recipients for their unwillingness to work – and the corollary assumption that they would earn their living easily if only they shook off their stupor and their habits of dependency – now sounds, is demonstrated by the fashion in which the Stock Exchange, that unwittingly sincere spokes-person for corporate interests, reacts to fluctuation in employment. It is not merely a question of the absence of any sign of Stock Exchange anxiety, let alone a panic reaction, when the rise of overall unemployment in a given country is accelerating; the Stock Exchange does react, and reacts enthusi-astically, to the news that employment is *not* likely to rise. The information that from June to July 1996 the number of new vacancies in the USA fell and the percentage of people officially out of work thereby rose, was reported under the title 'Employment Data Cheer Wall Street' (the Dow Jones gained 70 points in one day).[2] The value of shares in the giant con-glomerate AT&T rose dramatically on the day its managers announced the cutting of 40,000 jobs[3] – an experience repeated virtually daily on all Stock Exchanges around the world.

Just how nebulous, naïve or duplicitous, the idea of 'return to work' becomes, testifies to the profound change taking place in the very under-standing of 'prosperity' – and of 'good' and 'bad' tendency in economic life. In an authoritative depth analysis of the present state of large European corporations (under the title 'European Companies Gain from the Pain' and symptomatic subtitle 'Cost-cutting has led to profits, if not to jobs'; see *International Herald Tribune*, 17 November 1997), Tom Buerkle rejoices in the 'positive developments' in European economy:

> The sharply improved picture indicated that Europe Inc. is beginning to reap the rewards of painful restructuring efforts of recent years. Following the methods adopted by U.S. companies in the 1980s, many European firms have been shedding labour, closing or selling off what they consider nonessential businesses and streamlining management in a drive for greater profitability.

Profits indeed grow fast – the cause for the share-holders' rejoicing and the learned analysts' enthusiastic approval – despite the ostensibly less im-portant 'side effects' of the economic success. 'This newly robust corporate health is unlikely to reduce unemployment soon', Buerkle admits. Indeed, just in the last six years the manufacturing workforce shrank by 17.9 per cent in Britain, by 17.6 in Germany and 13.4 in France. In the U.S., where the 'positive developments' started around a decade earlier, the manufacturing labour shrank by 'only' 6.1 per cent. But solely because the flesh had been cut earlier almost to the bone . . .

Little wonder that according to the surveys of concerns, worries and fears of contemporary Europeans, joblessness – already suffered or threatened – occupies the uncontested topmost position. According to one such survey (by MORI) 85 per cent of Finns, 78 per cent of French and Swedes, 73 per cent of Germans and 72 per cent of Spaniards see unemployment as the most important problem of their countries. Let us recall that the criteria set for entry to European monetary union were set with the securing of a 'healthy economy' in mind, and that a falling rate of unemployment does not figure among these criteria. As a matter of fact, the desperate attempts to reach what passes today for the standard of 'economic health' are widely seen as the major obstacle against doing anything really effective to raise employment levels through job creation.

The apotheosis of work as simultaneously the highest human duty, the condition of moral decency, the guarantee of law and order and the cure for the plague of poverty, chimed in once with the labour-intensive industry which clamoured for more working hands in order to increase its product. The present-day streamlined, downsized, capital- and knowledge-intensive industry casts labour as a constraint on the rise of productivity. In direct defiance of the once canonical Smith/Ricardo/Marx labour theories of value, excess of labour is viewed as an anathema, and any search for more rationalization (i.e. more profit on the capital invested) focuses first on further possibilities to cut down the number of employees. 'Economic growth' and the rise of employment are, for all practical intents, at cross-purposes; technological progress is measured by the replacement and elimination of labour. Under such circumstances the commandments and blandishments of the work ethic sound increasingly hollow. They do not reflect any more the 'needs of industry' and can hardly be portrayed as the key to the 'wealth of the nation'. Their persistence, or rather their recent resuscitation in political discourse, can be only explained by some new functions which the work ethic is expected to perform in the post-industrial, consumer society of our times.

As Ferge and Miller suggest[4], the recent renaissance of work-ethic propaganda serves the 'separation of the deserving and non-deserving poor, putting the blame on the last, and justifying thereby society's indifference to them', and hence 'the acceptance of poverty as an inevitable plague due to personal defects, and an ensuing insensibility towards the poor and the deprived'. In other words, while no longer supplying the means to reduce poverty, the work ethic may yet help to reconcile society to the eternal presence of the poor, and allow society to live, more or less quietly and at peace with itself, in their presence.

The discovery of the 'underclass'

The term 'working class' belongs to the imagery of a society in which the tasks and functions of the better-off and the worse-off are divided – different but *complementary*. 'Working class' evokes an image of a class of people who have a role to play in the life of a society, who make a useful contribution to that society as a whole and expect to be rewarded accordingly.

The term 'lower class' belongs to the imagery of social mobility – of a society in which people are on the move and each position is but moment-ary and in principle amenable to change. 'Lower class' evokes an image of a class of people who stand or are cast at the bottom of a ladder which they may yet climb, and so exit from their present inferiority.

The term 'underclass' belongs to the imagery of a society which is not all-embracing and comprehensive, which is smaller than the sum of its parts. 'Underclass' evokes an image of a class of people who are beyond classes and outside hierarchy, with neither chance nor need of readmission; people without role, making no useful contribution to the lives of the rest, and in principle beyond redemption.

This is the inventory of people crowded together in the generic image of the underclass, described by Herbert J. Gans[5]:

> This behavioural definition denominates poor people who drop out of school, do not work, and, if they are young women, have babies without benefit of marriage and go on welfare. The behavioural underclass also includes the homeless, beggars, and panhandlers, poor addicts to alcohol and drugs[6], and street criminals. Because the term is flexible, poor people who live in 'the projects', illegal immigrants, and teenage gang members are often also assigned to the underclass. Indeed, the very flexibility of the behavioural definition is what lends itself to the term becoming a label that can be used to stigmatize poor people, whatever their actual behaviour.

An utterly heterogeneous and extremely variegated collection indeed. What can make putting them all together look sensible? What do single mothers have in common with alcoholics, or illegal immigrants with school dropouts?

One trait that does mark them all is that others see no good reason for their existence and may imagine themselves to be much better off if they were not around. People get cast in the underclass because they are seen as totally useless – something the rest of us could do nicely without. They are, indeed, blots on an otherwise pretty landscape, ugly yet greedy weeds, which add nothing to the harmonious beauty of the garden but suck out a lot of plant feed. Everyone would gain if they vanished.

And since they are all useless, the dangers they carry dominate the perception of them. The dangers are as varied as their carriers. They range from outright violence, murder and robbery lurking in a dark street, through nuisance and embarassment caused by the conscience-disturbing sight of human misery, to the 'drag on common resources'.[7] And where a danger is suspected, fear is quick to follow. 'Underclass' relates to people who are visible and prominent mostly for being feared; who *are* feared.

Uselessness and danger belong to the ample family of W.B. Gallie's 'essentially contested concepts'; when used as the criteria of designation they therefore display the 'flexibility' which makes the resulting classifications so exquisitely fit to accommodate all the most sinister demons haunting a society tormented by doubts about the durability of any usefulness, as well as by dispersed, un-anchored yet ambient fears. The mental map of the world drawn with their help provides an infinitely vast playground for successive 'moral panics'. The obtained divisions can be stretched with little effort to absorb and domesticate new threats, while at the same time allowing dissipated terrors to focus on a target which is reassuring just for being concrete.

This is, arguably, one – yet tremendously important – use which the uselessness of the underclass offers to a society in which no trade or profession can be any longer certain of its own long-term usefulness; and an important service, which the dangerousness of the underclass offers to a society convulsed by anxieties too numerous for it to be able to say with any degree of confidence what there is to be afraid of, and what is to be done to assuage the fear.

It was not perhaps merely by accident that the discovery of the underclass occurred at the time when the Cold War was grinding to a halt, losing fast much of its terror-generating power; and that the underclass debate came into full swing and settled in the centre of public attention once the 'Evil Empire' imploded and collapsed. The danger no longer threatens from outside; nor does it reside in the 'outside internalized' – foreign powers' internal footholds and bridgeheads, the fifth column implanted by the enemy from outside. The political threat of a foreign-fomented and trained revolution is no longer real and is difficult to make credible. But a sufficiently frightening substitute for the Soviet/Communist conspiracy is not in sight; while the occasional, scattered and often aimless acts of political terrorism arouse time and again fears about home-and-person safety, they are too sporadic and not sufficiently connected to congeal into a serious anxiety about the integrity of social order. Having nowhere else to strike roots, danger must reside now *inside* society and grow out of *local* soil. One is tempted to say that were there no underclass, it would have to be invented. As a matter of fact, it *has been* duly invented.

This does not mean, of course, that there are no beggars, drug-users and unwed mothers – the kind of 'miserable' or 'repugnant' people regularly pointed to whenever the existence of an underclass is questioned. It does mean, though, that their presence in society does not in the slightest suffice to prove the existence of the underclass. Plunging them all into one category is a *classificatory decision*, not the verdict of facts; condensing them into one entity, charging them all, collectively, with uselessness and with harbouring awesome dangers to the rest of society, is an exercise in *value-choice* and *evaluation*, not a description. Above all, while the idea of the underclass rests on the presumption that society (the totality which holds inside everything that makes it viable) may be smaller than the sum of its parts, the underclass *denoted* by the idea is *bigger* than the sum of its parts: the act of inclusion adds a new quality which no part on its own would possess. In reality, 'single mother' and an 'underclass woman' are *not* the same creatures. It takes a great deal of effort (though little thought) to make the first into the second.

The work ethic goes underclass

The word 'underclass' was first used by Gunnar Myrdal in 1963, to signal the dangers of de-industrialization, which – as he feared – was likely to make growing chunks of the population permanently unemployed and unemployable; not because of deficiencies or moral faults in the people who found themselves out of work, but purely and simply because of the lack of employment for all those who needed it and desired it. This was not the result of the work ethic failing to inspire, but of society's failure to guarantee life according to the work ethic's precepts. Members of the underclass, in Myrdal's sense, were victims of exclusion. Their new status was not the outcome of opting-out, and the exclusion was the product of economic logic, over which those earmarked for exclusion had no control and no influence.

The concept of the underclass burst into public attention much later, on 29 August 1977, via a cover story in *Time* magazine. And it did so carrying a quite different meaning: that of 'a large group of people who are more intractable, more socially alien and more hostile than almost anyone had imagined. They are the unreachables: the American underclass'. A long list followed this definition. It included juvenile delinquents, school dropouts, drug addicts, welfare mothers, looters, arsonists, violent criminals, unmarried mothers, pimps, pushers, panhandlers; all the names of decent people's overt fears and all the covert burdens of decent people's consciences.

'Intractable'. 'Alien'. 'Hostile'. And, as a result of all this, unreachable. No point in stretching out a helping hand – it would simply hang in the void. These people were beyond cure; and they were beyond cure because they had *chosen* a life of disease.

Unreachable meant also beyond the reach of the work ethic. Admonitions, blandishments, appeals to conscience would not pierce through the wall of voluntary alienation from everything which was dear to ordinary people. This was not just a question of refusal to work or of a preference for an idle and parasitic life, but of an open hostility to everything the work ethic stood for.

When Ken Auletta undertook in 1981–2 a series of exploratory excursions into the 'underclass' world, reported in the *New Yorker* and later collected in a widely read and highly influential book, he was prompted, by his own admission, by the anxiety felt by most of his fellow-citizens:

> I wondered: who are those people behind the bulging crime, welfare, and drug statistics – and the all-too-visible rise in antisocial behaviour – that afflicts most American cities? . . . I quickly learned that among students of poverty there is little disagreement that a fairly distinct black and white underclass does exist; that this underclass generally feels excluded from society, rejects commonly accepted values, suffers from *behavioural*, as well as *income* deficiencies. They don't just tend to be poor; to most Americans their behaviour seems aberrant.[8]

Note the vocabulary, the syntax, the rhetoric of the discourse within which the image of the underclass is generated and sustained. Auletta's text is perhaps the best site to study it, because unlike most of his less scrupulous successors Auletta does not engage in simple 'underclass bashing'; on the contrary, he leans over backwards to retain and manifest his objectivity, and pities as much as condemns the negative heroes of his story.[9]

Note 'bulging crime' and 'bulging welfare', as well as welfare and drug statistics, are mentioned in one breath and set at the same level. Thus no argument, let alone proof, is needed to explain why they have found themselves in each other's neighbourhood and why they have all been classed as instances of the same 'antisocial' behaviour. One need not take the risky step of pointing out explicitly that drug-pushing and being on welfare are similarly antisocial, are afflictions of the same order; the implicit suggestion to this effect (which would surely raise a few eyebrows if made explicit) has been achieved by a purely syntactic stratagem.

Note as well that the underclass *rejects* common values, but it only *feels* excluded. The underclass is the active and acting, action-generating, initiative-taking side in a two-sided relationship that has 'most Americans' as the other protagonist; it is the behaviour of the underclass, and of the underclass alone, that comes under critical scrutiny and is declared aberrant. On the other hand it is 'most Americans' who, of right, sit in judgment, but it is the actions of the underclass that are judged. If not for its antisocial deeds, the underclass would not be brought to court. Most importantly, however, there would then be no need for the court's session, since there would be no case to ponder, no crime to punish nor negligence to repair.

The rhetoric is followed by practices, from which it gets retrospective confirmation and draws the arguments it might have been short of when first used. The more ample and widespread such practices, the more self-evident sound the suggestions which triggered them and the less chance there is of the rhetorical subterfuge ever being spotted, let alone objected to. Most of Auletta's empirical material was drawn from the Wildcat Skills Training Centre, an institution established with the noble intention of re-habilitating and restoring to society the acknowledged members of the underclass. Who was eligible for admission? Four qualifications gave an equal right to be trained at the Centre. A candidate had to be a fairly recent prison convict or an ex-addict still undergoing treatment, a female on welfare, without children under the age of 6, or a youth between 17 and 20 who had dropped out of school. Whoever set the rules of admission must have decided beforehand that these four 'types', so distinct to an untrained eye, suffered from the same kind of problem, or rather *presented* the same kind of problem and therefore needed the same kind of treatment. What started as the rule-setters' decision, however, must have turned into the Wildcat Centre students' reality: for a considerable time they were put in each other's company, subjected to the same regime, and instructed daily as to the commonality of their fate. And being inside the Wildcat Centre supplied for the duration all the social definition they needed and could reasonably work for. Once more word had become flesh.[10]

Auletta is at pains to remind his readers time and again that 'underclassness' is not a matter of poverty, or, at least, that it cannot be explained solely by it. He points out that of 25–29 million Americans officially below the poverty line, only an 'estimated 9 million do not assimilate'[11] and 'operate outside the generally accepted boundaries of society', set apart as they are 'by their "deviant" or antisocial behaviour'[12]. The implicit suggestion is that the elimination of poverty, were it at all conceivable, would not put an end to the underclass phenomenon. If one may be poor and yet 'operate within accepted boundaries', then factors other than poverty must be responsible for descending into the underclass. These factors were seen to be psychological and behavioural afflictions, made perhaps more frequent under conditions of poverty, but not determined by it.

According to this suggestion, descent into the underclass is a matter of choice – deliberate or by default. It is a choice even if a person falls into the underclass simply because they fail or neglect to do what is needed to extricate themselves from poverty. Not doing what is needed, in a country of free choosers, is easily, without a second thought, interpreted as choosing something else instead – in this case 'unsocial behaviour'. Falling into the underclass is an exercise in freedom. In a society of free consumers curbing one's freedom is impermissible; but so is, many would say, *not* curtailing the freedom of people who use their freedom to abridge other people's freedoms, by accosting, pestering, threatening, fun-spoiling, burdening consciences and otherwise making other people's lives nasty.

Separating the 'problem of the underclass' from the 'issue of poverty' is like hitting several birds with one stone. Its most obvious effect is – in a society famous for its love of litigation – to deny the people assigned to the underclass the right to 'claim damages' by presenting themselves as victims of societal malfunction. In whatever litigation may follow their case, the burden of proof will be shifted fairly and squarely onto the 'underclassers'. It is they who must take the first step and prove their goodwill and determination to be good. Whatever is to be done must be done in the first place by the underclassers themselves (though of course there is no shortage of professional and self-appointed counsellors to advise them as to what it is exactly that they must do). If nothing happens and the spectre of the underclass refuses to go away, the explanation is simple; it is also clear who is to blame. If the rest of society has something to reproach itself for it is only for its insufficient determination to curtail the underclassers iniquitous choices. More police, more prisons, ever more severe and frightening punishments, seem then the most obvious means to repair the mistake.

Perhaps more seminal yet is another effect: the abnormality of the underclass phenomenon 'normalizes' the issue of poverty. It is the underclass which is placed outside the accepted boundaries of society, but the underclass constitutes, as we remember, only a fraction of the 'officially poor'. It is precisely because the underclass is such a big and urgent problem that the bulk of people living in poverty are not a great issue that needs to be urgently tackled. Against the background of the uniformly ugly and repulsive landscape of the underclass, the 'merely poor' shine as temporarily unlucky but essentially decent people who – unlike the underclassers – will make all the right choices and eventually find their way back into the accepted boundaries of society. Just as falling into the underclass and staying there is a matter of choice, so the rehabilitation from the state of poverty is also a matter of choice – the right choice this time. The tacit suggestion conveyed by the idea that the descent of a poor person into the underclass is the outcome of choice, is that another choice may accomplish the opposite and lift the poor from their social degradation.

A central and largely uncontested – since unwritten – rule of a consumer society is that being free to choose requires competence: skill and determination to use the power of choice. Freedom to choose does not mean that all choices are right – there are good and bad choices, better and worse choices. The kind of choice made is the evidence of competence or its lack. The underclass is the aggregate product of wrong individual choices; proof of the 'choice incompetence' of its members.

In his highly influential tract on the roots of present-day poverty[13], Lawrence C. Mead singles out that incompetence as the paramount cause of the persistence of poverty amid affluence, and of the sordid failure of all successive state-run policies meant to eliminate it. The poor purely and simply lack the competence to appreciate the advantages of working life; they make wrong choices, putting 'nowork' above work. It is because of that incompetence, says Mead, that the invocation of the work ethic falls on deaf ears and fails to influence the choices of the poor:

> The issue hinges on whether the needy can be responsible for themselves and, above all, on whether they have the competence to manage their lives . . .[14] Whatever outward causes one cites, a mystery in the heart of nowork remains – the *passivity* of the seriously poor in seizing the opportunities that apparently exist for them . . . To explain nowork, I see no avoiding some appeal to psychology or culture. Mostly, seriously poor adults appear to avoid work, not because of their economic situation, but because of what they believe . . .[15] In the absence of prohibitive barriers to employment, the question of the personality of the

poor emerges as the key to understanding and overcoming poverty. Psychology is the last frontier in the search for the causes of low work effort . . . Why do the poor not seize [the opportunities] as assiduously as the culture assumes they will? *Who exactly are they?*[16] The core of the culture of poverty seems to be inability to control one's life – what psychologists call inefficacy.[17]

The opportunities are there; are not all of us the walking proof of that? But opportunities must be also seen as such, and embraced, and that takes competence: some wits, some will and some effort. The poor obviously lack all three. This impairment of the poor is, all things considered, good, reassuring news. We are responsible, offering the poor opportunities. The poor are irresponsible, refusing to take them. Just like the medics who reluctantly throw in the towel when their patients consistently refuse to cooperate with the prescribed treatment, we all may as well give up our efforts to provide job opportunities in the face of the stubborn reluctance of the poor to work. There are limits to what we can do. The teachings of the work ethic are available to anyone who will listen, and opportunities to work wait to be seized – the rest is up to the poor themselves. They have no right to demand anything else from us.

If poverty continues to exist and grow amidst growing affluence, the work ethic must have been ineffective. But if we believe that it stays ineffective only because its commandments are not properly listened to and obeyed, then this failure to listen and obey can only be explained by either moral defectiveness or criminal intent on the part of those who fall out.

Let me repeat: in the beginning, the work ethic was a highly effective means of filling up factories hungry for more labour. With labour turning fast into an obstacle to higher productivity, the work ethic still has a role to play, but this time as an effective means to wash clean all the hands and consciences inside the accepted boundaries of society of the guilt of abandoning a large number of their fellow citizens to permanent redundancy. Purity of hands and consciences is reached by the twin measure of the moral condemnation of the poor and the moral absolution of the rest.

To be poor is criminal

Mead's pamphlet against the poor who 'have chosen' not to work for their living ends with an emphatic invocation: 'Social policy must resist passive poverty justly and firmly – much as the West contained communism – until sanity breaks in and the opposed system collapses of its own weight'[18]. The metaphor is faultlessly chosen. One of the foremost services that the underclass renders to the present-day affluent society is the sucking-in of the fears and anxieties no longer drained by a potent enemy outside. The underclass is the enemy inside the walls, destined to replace the external enemy as a drug crucial to collective sanity; a safety valve for collective tensions born of individual insecurity.

The underclass is particularly well fit to play this role. Mead says repeatedly that what prods 'normal', decent Americans to form a united front against the welfare spongers, criminals and school dropouts, is what they perceive as the dire inconsistency of those they unite against: the underclassers offend all the cherished values of the majority while clinging to them and desiring the same joys of consumer life as other people boast to have *earned*. In other words, what Americans hold against the underclass in their midst is that its dreams and the model of life it desires are so uncannily similar to their own. And yet the similarity can hardly be seen as a matter of inconsistency. As Peter Townsend pointed out, it is the logic of a consumer society to mould its poor as unfulfilled consumers: 'consumer lifestyles are becoming increasingly inaccessible to those on the low incomes defined historically in terms of a fixed purchasing value of subsistence or basic needs'[19]. However, it is precisely that inaccessibility of consumer lifestyles that the consumer society trains its members to experience as the most painful of deprivations.

Every type of social order produces some visions of the dangers which threaten its identity. But each society spawns visions made to its own measure – to the measure of the kind of social order it struggles to achieve. On the whole, these visions tend to be mirror images of the society which spawns them, while images of threat tend to be self-portraits of the society with minus signs. Or, to put this in psychoanalytical terms, threats are projections of a society's own inner ambivalence about its own ways and means; about the fashion in which it lives and perpetuates its living. A society unsure about the survival of its mode of being develops the mentality of a besieged fortress. The enemies who lay siege to its walls are its own, very own 'inner demons', the suppressed, ambient fears which permeate its daily life, its 'normality', yet which, in order to make the daily reality endurable, must be squashed and squeezed out of the lived-through quotidianity and moulded into an alien body: into a tangible enemy whom one can fight, and fight again, and even hope to conquer.

In line with this universal rule, the danger which haunted the classic, order-building and order-obsessed modern state was that of the revolution. The enemies were the revolutionaries, or, rather, the hot-headed, harebrained, all-too-radical reformists, the subversive forces trying to replace the extant state-managed order with another state-managed order, with a counter-order reversing each and any principle by which the present order lived or aimed to live.

The self-image of social order has changed since those times and so the image of the threat – the image of order with a minus sign – has acquired a new shape. Whatever has been registered in recent years as rising criminality (a process, let us note, which happened to run parallel to the falling membership of the Communist or other radical parties of 'alternative order'), is not a product of malfunction or neglect, but consumer society's own product, logically (if not legally) legitimate. What is more, it is also its inescapable product. The higher is the consumer demand (that is, the more effective is the market seduction) the more is the consumer society safe and prosperous. Yet, simultaneously, the wider and deeper does the gap grow between those who desire and can satisfy their desires (those who have been seduced and proceed to act in the way the state of being seduced prompts them to act), and those who have been seduced and yet are unable to act in the way the seduced are expected to act. Market seduction is, simultaneously, the great equalizer and the great divider. To be effective, the enticement to consume, and to consume more, must be transmitted in all directions and addressed indiscriminately to everybody who will listen. But more people can listen than can respond in the fashion which the seductive message was meant to elicit. Those who cannot act on the desires so induced are treated daily to the dazzling spectacle of those who can. Lavish consumption, they are told, is the sign of success, a highway leading straight to public applause and fame. They also learn that possessing and consuming certain objects and practising certain lifestyles is the necessary condition of happiness; perhaps even of human dignity.

If consumption is the measure of a successful life, of happiness and even of human decency, then the lid has been taken off human desires; no amount of acquisitions and exciting sensations is likely ever to bring satisfaction in the way the 'keeping up to the standards' once promised: there are no standards to keep up to. The finishing line moves forward together with the runner, the goals keep forever a step or two ahead as one tries to reach them. Records keep being broken, and there seems to be no end to what a human may desire. Dazzled and baffled, people learn that in the newly privatized, and thus 'liberated' companies which they remember as austere public institutions constantly famished for cash, the present managers draw salaries measured in millions, while those sacked from their managerial chairs are indemnified, again in millions of pounds, for their botched and sloppy work. From all places, through all communication channels, the message comes loud and clear: there are no standards except that of grab-bing more, and no rules, except the imperative of 'playing one's cards right'.

However, no card game hands are even. If winning is the sole object of the game, those who got a poor hand are tempted to try whatever other re-sources they can muster. From the point of view of the casino owners, some resources – those that they themselves allocate or circulate – are legal tender; all other resources, though, those beyond their control, are prohibited. The line dividing the fair from the unfair does not look the same, however, from the side of the players, particularly from the side of the would-be, aspiring players, and most particularly from the side of the incapacitated aspiring players, who do not have access to the legal tender. They may resort to the resources they *do* have, whether recognized as legal or declared illegal, or opt out of the game altogether. That latter move, however, has been made, by market seduction, all but impossible to contemplate.

The disarming, disempowering and suppressing of unfulfilled players is therefore an indispensable supplement to integration-through-seduction in a market-led society of consumers. The impotent, indolent players are to be kept outside the game. They are the waste-product of the game, a waste product which the game cannot stop spitting out without grinding to a halt and calling in the receivers. The game would not benefit from halting the production of waste for another reason: those who stay in the game need to be shown the horrifying sight of the (sole and only, as they are told) alternative, in order to make them able and willing to endure the hardships and the tensions that their lives lived in the game gestate.

Given the nature of the game now played, the misery of those left out of it, once treated as a collectively caused blight which needed to be dealt with by collective means, can be only redefined as an individual crime. The 'dangerous classes' are thus redefined as classes of criminals. And so the prisons fully and truly deputize now for the fading welfare institutions, and in all probability will have to do this to a growing extent as welfare provisions continue to taper.

The growing incidence of behaviour classified as criminal is not an obstacle on the road to a fully-fledged and all-embracing consumerist society. On the contrary, it is its natural accompaniment and prerequisite. This is so, admittedly, for a number of reasons, but the main reason among them is perhaps the fact that those left out of the game – the unfulfilled consumers, whose resources do not measure up to their desires, and who have therefore little or no chance of winning while playing the game by its official rules – are the living incarnation of the 'inner demons' specific to consumer life. Their ghettoization and criminalization, the severity of the sufferings administered to them and the overall cruelty of the fate visited upon them, are – metaphorically speaking – the ways of exorcizing such inner demons and burning them out in effigy. The criminalized margins serve as soi-disant tools of sanitation: the sewers into which the inevitable, but poisonous effluvia of consumerist seduction are disposed, so that the people who manage to stay in the game of consumerism need not worry about the state of their own health. If this is, however the prime stimulus of the present exuberance of what the great Norwegian criminologist Nils Christie called 'the prison industry'[20], then the hope that the process can be slowed down, let alone halted or reversed in a thoroughly deregulated and privatized society animated and run by the consumer market, is – to say the least – slight.

Nowhere is the connection exposed more fully than in the United States, where the unqualified rule of the consumer market reached, in the years of Reagan-Bush free-for-all, further than in any other country. The years of deregulation and dismantling of welfare provisions were also the years of rising criminality, of a growing police force and prison population. They were also the years in which an ever more gory and spectacularly cruel lot needed to be reserved for those declared criminal, in order to match the fast-growing fears and anxieties, nervousness and uncertainty, anger and fury of the silent or not-so-silent majority of ostensibly successful consumers. The more powerful became the 'inner demons', the more insatiable grew the desire of the majority to see the crime punished and justice done. The liberal Bill Clinton won the presidential election promising to multiply the ranks of the police and build new and more secure prisons. Some observers (among them Peter Linebaugh of the University of Toledo, Ohio, the author of *The London Hanged*) believe that Clinton owed his election to the widely publicized execution of a retarded man, Ricky Ray Rector, whom he allowed to go to the electric chair when the Governor of Arkansas. Two years later Clinton's opponents in the radical right sections of the Republican Party swept the board in the congressional elections having convinced the electorate that Clinton had not done enough to fight criminality and that they would do more. The second election of Clinton was won in a campaign in which both candidates tried to out-shout and overtake each other in their promises of a strong police force and no mercy for all those who 'offend society's values while clinging to them' – who make a bid for the consumerist life without proper credentials and without contributing to the perpetuation of consumer society.

In 1972, just as the welfare era reached its summit and just before its fall began, the Supreme Court of the United States, mirroring the public mood of the time, ruled the death penalty to be arbitrary and capricious, and as such unfit to serve the cause of justice. Several other rulings later, the Court in 1988 permitted the execution of 16-year-olds, in 1989 the execution of the mentally retarded, and finally in 1992 in the infamous case of Herrera vs. Collins it ruled that the accused may be innocent, but still could be executed if trials were properly conducted and constitutionally correct. The recent Crime Bill passed by the Senate and the House of Representatives extends the number of offences punishable by death to 57 or even, according to certain interpretations, 70. With high publicity and a lot of fanfare, a federal state-of-the-art execution chamber with a death row planned to hold 120 convicts, was built at the US penitentiary in Terre Haute, Indiana. At the beginning of 1994, altogether 2802 people were awaiting execution in American prisons. Of these, 1102 were Afro-American, while 33 were sentenced to death when juveniles. The overwhelming majority of death-row inmates comes, expectedly, from that huge and growing warehouse where the failures and the rejects of consumer society are stored. As Linebaugh suggests, the spectacle of execution is 'cynically used by politicians to terrorize a growing underclass'. In demanding the terrorization of the underclass, the silent American majority attempts to terrorize away its own inner terrors.

According to Herbert Gans, 'the feelings harboured by the more fortunate classes about the poor [are a] mixture of fear, anger and disapproval, but fear may be the most important element in the mixture'.[21] Indeed, the emotionally-loaded mixture of sentiments may be motivationally and politically effective only in so far as the fear is intense and truly terrifying. The widely advertised defiance of the work ethic by the poor and their reluctance to share in the hard work of the decent majority, is enough to cause widespread anger and disapproval. When, however, the image of the idle poor is overlaid with the alarming news of rising criminality and violence against the lives and property of the decent majority, disapproval is topped up by fear; non-obedience to the work ethic becomes a *fearful* act, in addition to being morally odious and repulsive.

Poverty turns then from the subject matter of social policy into a problem for penology and criminal law. The poor are no longer the rejects of consumer society, defeated in the all-out competitive wars; they are the outright enemies of society. There is but a tenuous and easily crossed line dividing the recipients of welfare from drug-pushers, robbers and murderers. People on welfare are the natural catchment area for criminal gangs, and keeping people on welfare means enlarging the pool from which the criminals are recruited.

Expulsion from the universe of moral obligations

Linking poverty with criminality has another effect: it helps to banish the poor from the universe of moral obligations.

The substance of morality is the impulse of responsibility for the integrity and well-being of other people who are weak, unfortunate and suffering; criminalization of poverty tends to extinguish and argue away that impulse. As actual or potential criminals, the poor cease to be an ethical problem – they are exempt from our moral responsibility. There is no more a moral question of defending the poor against the cruelty of their fate; instead, there is the ethical question of defending the right and proper lives of decent people against the assaults likely to be plotted in mean streets, ghettos and no-go areas.

As has been said before, since in the present-day society the non-working poor are no more the 'reserve army of labour', there is no *economic* sense in keeping them in good shape just in case they are called back to active service as producers. This does not by itself mean, though, that there is no *moral* sense in providing them with conditions of dignified human existence. Their well-being may not be relevant to the struggle for productivity and profitability, but it is still crucially relevant to the moral sentiments and concerns owed to human beings as well as the self-esteem of the human community. Gans begins his book with a quotation from Thomas Paine:

> When it shall be said in any country in the world, my poor are happy; neither ignorance nor distress is to be found among them; my jails are empty of prisoners, my streets of beggars; the aged are not in want, the taxes are not oppressive . . . ; when these things can be said, then may that country boast of its constitution and its government.

In the early stages of modern history the work ethic had the distinct advantage of linking economic interests to the ethical concerns of the kind spelled out by Thomas Paine. Bringing the poor to the factory to work might have served the interests of the producers and merchandisers of goods (and these interests might even have supplied most vigour to the propaganda of the work ethic) but it also appealed to the moral sensitivity of the public, worried, disturbed and ashamed by the sight of human misery suffered by the unemployed. Given the seemingly insatiable thirst of emerging mass industry for an ever-growing supply of labour, moral concerns could seek a legitimate and realistic outlet in spreading the gospel of the work ethic. There was, one might say, a historically occasioned encounter between the interests of capital and the moral sentiments of society at large.

This being no longer the case, the ostensibly unchanged message of the work ethic has entered a new kind of relationship with public morality. It is no longer an outlet for moral sentiments; instead, it has become a powerful instrument of the late-twentieth-century version of 'adiaphorization' – the process whereby the ethical opprobrium is taken away from morally repugnant acts.

To 'adiaphorize' an action is to declare it morally neutral, or rather make it subject to assessment by other than moral criteria while being exempt from moral evaluation. The call to abide by the commandments of the work ethic serves now as a test of eligibility for moral empathy. Most of those to whom the appeal is addressed are expected (bound) to fail this test, and once they fail they can be without compunction assumed to have put themselves, by their own choice, outside the realm of moral obligation. Society can now relinquish all further responsibility for their predicament without feeling guilty about abandoning its ethical duty. No mean achievement, given the pervasiveness of moral impulse and the spontaneous, common sensitivity to human misery, pain, suffering and humiliation.

The stifling of moral impulse can never be complete, and so the exile from the universe of moral obligations cannot be absolute. However successfully consciences may be silenced by persistent bombardment with the news of moral depravity and criminal inclinations of the non-working poor, the indissoluble residues of moral impulse must be given, time and again, an outlet. Such an outlet is provided by periodical 'carnivals of charity' – massive but as a rule short-lived explosions of pent-up moral feelings triggered by lurid sights of particularly hideous sufferings and particularly devastating misery. As all carnivals, however, are meant to obliquely reinforce, not to undermine, the rules of quotidianity, the spectacles of mass charity render day-to-day equanimity and moral indifference more bearable; in the end, they fortify the beliefs which justify the ethical exile of the poor.

As Ryszard Kapuściński, one of the most formidable chronographers of contemporary living, has recently explained, that effect is achieved by three interconnected expedients consistently applied by the media who preside over these 'charity fairs'.[22]

First, the news of a successive famine or another wave of uprooting and enforced homelessness come as a rule coupled with the reminder that the same distant lands where the people 'as seen on TV' die of famine and disease are the birthplace of 'Asian tigers'. It does not matter that all the 'tigers' together embrace no more than one per cent of the population of Asia alone. They are assumed to demonstrate what needs to be proved

– that the sorry plight of the hungry and the homeless is their *sui generis* choice. Alternatives are available, but not taken as a result of lack of industry or resolve. The underlying message is that the poor themselves bear responsibility for their fate. They could, as the 'tigers' did, choose a life of work and thrift instead.

Second, such news is so scripted and edited as to reduce the problem of poverty and deprivation to the question of hunger alone. This stratagem has two effects: the real scale of poverty is played down (800 million people are permanently undernourished, but something like 4 billion, two thirds of the world population, live in poverty), and the task ahead is limited to finding food for the hungry. But, as Kapuściński points out, such a presentation of the problem of poverty (as exemplified by a recent issue of *The Economist* analysing world poverty under the heading 'How to Feed the World'), 'terribly degrades, virtually denies full humanity to people whom we want, allegedly, to help'. The equation 'poverty = hunger' conceals many other complex aspects of poverty: 'horrible living and housing conditions, illness, illiteracy, aggression, falling apart families, weakening of social bonds, lack of future and non-productiveness'. These are afflictions which cannot be cured with high-protein biscuits and powdered milk. Kapuściński remembers wandering through African townships and villages and meeting children 'who begged me not of bread, water, chocolate or toys, but a ballpen, since they went to school and had nothing to write their lessons with'.

Let us add that all associations between the horrid pictures of famine as presented by the media and the plight of the poor accused of violating the principles of the work ethic are carefully avoided. People are shown, along with their hunger, but however much viewers strain their eyes, they cannot see a single worktool, plot of arable land or head of cattle in the picture. It is as if there is no connection between the emptiness of the work ethic's promises in a world which needs no more labour, and the plight of these people, offered as an outlet for pent-up moral impulses. The work ethic emerges from this exercise unscathed, ready to be used again as a whip to chase the poor nearer home away from the shelter they seek (in vain) in the welfare state.

Third, spectacles of disasters, as presented by the media, support and reinforce the ordinary, daily moral withdrawal in another way. Apart from unloading the accumulated supplies of moral sentiments, their long-term effect is that:

> the developed part of the world surrounds itself with a sanitary belt of uncommitment, erects a global Berlin Wall; all the information coming from 'out there' is pictures of war, murders, drugs, looting, contagious diseases, refugees and hunger; that is, of something threatening us.

Only rarely, and in half-voice, and in no connection with the scenes of civil wars and massacres, do we hear of the murderous weapons used, and even less often are we reminded of what we know but prefer not to be told about: that all those weapons used to make far-away homelands into killing fields have been supplied by our arms factories, jealous of their order books and proud of their competitiveness – that lifeblood of our own cherished prosperity. A synthetic image of self-inflicted brutality sediments itself into public consciousness; an image of 'mean streets' and 'no-go areas' writ large, a magnified rendition of a gangland, an alien, sub-human world beyond ethics and beyond salvation. Attempts to save that world from the worst consequences of its own brutality may only bring momentary effects and in the long run are bound to fail; all the lifelines thrown will be surely re-twisted into more nooses.

And then the well-tried, trusty tool of adiaphorization comes into its own: the sober, rational calculation of costs and effects. Money spent on these kinds of people is money wasted. And wasting money is one thing which, as everybody will readily agree, we cannot afford. Neither the victims of famine as ethical subjects, nor our own stance towards them is a moral issue. Morality is for carnivals only – those spectacular, instantaneous, yet short-lived, explosive condensations of pity and compassion. When it comes to our (the affluents') collective responsibility for the continuing misery of the world's poor, economic calculation takes over, and the rules of free trade, competitiveness and productivity replace ethical precepts. Where economy speaks, ethics had better keep silent.

Unless, of course, it is the *work* ethic, the sole variant that economic rules tolerate. The work ethic is not an adversary of economy bent on profitability and competitiveness, but its necessary and welcome supplement. For the affluent part of the world and the affluent sections of well-off societies, the work ethic is a one-sided affair. It spells out the duties of those who struggle with the task of survival; it says nothing about the duties of those who rose above mere survival and went on to more elevated, loftier concerns. In particular, it denies the dependency of the first upon the second, and so releases the second from responsibility for the first.

Today, the work ethic is instrumental in bringing the idea of 'dependency' into disrepute. Dependency is, increasingly, a dirty word. The welfare state is accused of cultivating dependency, of raising it to the level of self-perpetuating culture, and this is a crowning argument for dismantling it. Moral responsibility is the first victim of this holy war against dependency, as dependency of the 'Other' is but a mirror image of one's own responsibility, the starting point of any moral relationship and the founding assumption of all moral action. While denigrating dependency of the poor as sin, the work ethic in its present rendition brings most relief to the moral scruples of the affluent.

PART THREE

5

Prospects for the new poor

○───

There are many ways of being human, but each society makes a choice of the way it prefers or tolerates. If we call a certain assembly of people a 'society', implying that these people 'belong together' and make a 'totality', it is because of this choice. (Though seldom a 'deliberate' choice in the sense of surveying a number of possibilities and then picking the most appealing among them; once made by default rather than by design, the choice cannot be easily abandoned.[1]) It is this choice, or the lasting sediments of it, that makes one assembly of people look different from another; the difference which we refer to when we speak of different societies. Whether a given assembly is or is not a 'society', where its boundaries run, and who does and who does not belong to the society which that assembly constitutes, all depends on the force with which the choice is made and promoted, the strength of the grip in which it holds the individuals and the compliance with which it is obeyed. The choice boils down to two impositions (or, rather, one imposition with two effects): order and a norm.

The great novelist and philosopher of our times, Milan Kundera, described in *La Valse au Adieux* (Galimard, 1976[2]) 'the longing for order' evident in all known societies as:

> a desire to turn the human world into an inorganic one, where everything would function perfectly and work on schedule, subordinated to a suprapersonal system. The longing for order is at the same time a longing for death, because life is an incessant disruption of order. Or to put it the other way around: the desire for order is a virtuous pretext, an excuse for violent misanthropy.

As a matter of fact, the desire for order does not necessarily stem from misanthropy. Yet it cannot but prompt it, since it offers an excuse for whatever actions could be dictated by such a sentiment. In the last account,

any order is a desperate attempt to impose uniformity, regularity and pre-
dictability on the human world, and humans are inclined to be diversified,
erratic and unpredictable. Since humans are, as Cornelius Castoriadis put
it, 'one type of being that creates something else, that is a source of alterity,
and that thereby itself alters itself',[3] there is but a meagre chance that the
human world anywhere (except for the graveyards) will ever cease to be
diversified, erratic and unpredictable. Being human means constant choice
and reversibility of all choice, and arresting further choice, rendering the
choice already made irreversible, takes some considerable effort. The longing for order is conceivable only thanks to that 'choosing quality' of being;
any model of order is itself a choice, but it is a choice that wants to super-
sede all other choices and put an end to all further choosing. Such an end is
not on the cards, though – misanthropy follows, whether intended and
welcome or not. The true object of suspicion, revulsion and hatred, of the
sentiments or attitudes which combine into misanthropy, is the stubborn,
inveterate and incurable eccentricity of human beings, that inexhaustible
source of disorder.

The other imposition is that of the norm. The norm is the projection of
the model of order upon human conduct. The norm tells what it means
to behave in an orderly fashion in a well-ordered society; it translates, so
to speak, the concept of order into the language of human choices. If any
order is a choice, so is the norm; but the choice of a certain kind of order
limits the choice of tolerable behavioural patterns. It privileges certain kinds
of conduct as normal, while casting all other kinds as abnormal. 'Abnormal'
stands for any departure from the favoured pattern; it can extend into 'deviation', an extreme form of abnormality. Deviation will trigger therapeutic
or penal intervention if the conduct in question does not just disagree with
the preferred pattern, but transcends the boundary of tolerable choices. The
distinction between mere abnormality and the much more sinister deviation
is never clearly drawn and as a rule is hotly contested, as is the question
of the limits to tolerance, being the attitude which defines the difference
between them.

A conscious concern with order and norm – the very fact that such
things are an issue and are discussed in a society – signals, as a rule, that not
everything is as it should be and that things cannot be left in their present
state. The very concepts of order and norm (concepts which, once they are
coined, allow one to see the problem of order and norm, to classify elements of the world as relevant to the issue of order and norm) are born of
that sense of imperfection of the current state of affairs and the urge to do
something about it. Both concepts are therefore 'positive' and 'constructive': they prod and press towards lifting reality to certain standards not yet
fully reached. Speaking of order and norm is in itself a powerful tool of
their imposition.

But the 'should' which they imply cuts into the 'is', leaving out large
chunks of human reality. Neither of the two ideas would make any sense
were they all-inclusive, able to accommodate all people and all the things

people do. The whole point about order and norm is exactly the opposite: the emphatic declaration that not everything that exists at present can be included in a postulated, properly functioning assembly and not every choice can be accommodated. The concepts of order and norm are sharp knives pressed against society as it *is*; they signal first and foremost the intent of separation, amputation, excision, expurgation and exclusion. They promote the 'proper' by focusing attention on the 'improper'; they single out, circumscribe and stigmatize those parts of reality which are denied the right to exist, and are destined for isolation, exile or extinction.

Installing and promoting order means performing the job of exclusion directly, by enforcing a special regime upon those meant to be excluded, excluding them by subordinating them to that special regime. Norm, on the other hand (any norm, the norms of the work ethic being just a specimen from a large class) acts indirectly, making the exclusion look more like self-marginalization.

In the first case, those who end up excluded and banished are people who 'breach the order'. In the second, it is those who are 'not up to the norm'. In both cases, though, the excluded themselves are charged with the guilt of their exclusion; the perspectives of order and norm alike apportion the blame in advance, decide the issue of πασχειν (suffering) versus ποιειν (doing) a priori against the excluded. It is the actions of the excluded marked for exclusion – *wrong* actions – that brings the plight of exclusion upon them. In the process of exclusion, the excluded themselves are the agency, the active side. Being excluded is thus represented as an outcome of social suicide, not social execution. It is the fault of the excluded that they did nothing, or not enough, to escape exclusion; perhaps they even invited their fate, making the exclusion into a foregone conclusion. Excluding them is not just an exercise in house-cleaning, but an ethical act, the apportioning of right deserts, an act of justice; those who decide and execute the exclusion can feel righteous, as becomes the defenders of law and order and the guardians of the values and standards of decency.

What these perspectives leave out of sight and prevent from being considered is the possibility that, far from bearing responsibility for their own sorry fate, the excluded might be at the receiving end of forces they have been given no chance of resisting, let alone controlling. It is possible that some among the excluded have 'breached the order' because of what they are or have been made. They are excluded because of traits they possess but did not choose to have, not because of what they have done but because 'people like them' do not fit into someone else's sense of order. Others among the excluded may not be 'up to the norm' not because of a lack of will, but due to the lack of resources without which living up to the norm is simply not possible – resources other people have, but they do not; resources which are in short supply and therefore cannot be had by all in sufficient measure.

Therefore it has been demonstrated that the excluded or about to be excluded are unfit to be free agents. Allowing them to be so will be their undoing. Horrid things will follow if they are let loose. They bring all sorts of disasters upon themselves. But since being excluded is not a state one is likely to enjoy, the consequences of their assumed freedom are as awful for the excluded themselves as they are for those who are orderly and within the norm. Depriving the excluded of their freedom to act (which they are bound to misuse or waste), is a move undoubtedly required for the protection of law and order, and can also be argued to be in the best interests of the excluded. Policing, controlling and supervising the conduct of the excluded is perceived as an act of charity, an ethical duty. These two aspects intertwine and merge into the urge to 'do something' about the substandard part of the population, an impulse which draws its strength from the concern with the installation and preservation of order yet invokes the support of the moral sentiments of pity and compassion. Whatever its animating force, however, that impulse rebounds as a rule in the efforts to 'heteronomize', to disempower, those who know not how to use their powers properly; to subordinate them, by hook or by crook, to the 'supra-personal system' which they evade or defy.

Since time immemorial, the two aspects of the defence of order and of compassion have combined and blended in the social construction of the figure of the poor. The poor are such people as are not fed, shod and clad as the standards of their time and place define as right and proper; but they are above all people who do not live 'up to the norm', that norm being the ability to meet such standards.

The poor without role

Every society known so far had its poor. And no wonder, since, let me repeat, the imposition of any model of order is a divisive act and disqualifies certain parts of social reality as unfitting or dysfunctional, while the promotion of any particular mode of being to the status of norm demotes a variety of alternative ways to the category of below par and abnormal. The poor are the very epitome and the prototype of the 'unfitting' and 'abnormal'.

Each known society took towards its poor a characteristically ambivalent attitude, an uneasy mixture of fear and revulsion on the one hand and pity and compassion on the other. Both ingredients were equally indispensable. The first allowed for harsh treatment of the poor of the kind which the defence of order required; the second underlined the pitiful lot of those who fell below the standards, a lot that made all the hardships of norm-following by the norm-abiding part of the population pale into insignificance. In such an oblique, roundabout way, the poor could be found, after all and despite everything, a useful role to play in the reproduction of social order and the effort to protect obedience to the norm.

Depending on its specific model of order and norm, however, each society constructed its poor in its own image, offering different explanations of their presence, finding a different use for the poor and deploying different strategies of tackling the problem of poverty.

Pre-modern Europe came closer than its modern successor to finding an important function for its poor. The poor, like everybody else and every-thing else in pre-modern Christian Europe, were Children of God – an indispensable link in the 'divine chain of beings'; a part of God's creation and, like the rest of the world before its modern desacralization or 'disen-chantment', saturated with meaning and purpose. The poor suffered, and their suffering was the repentance for original sin and a warrant of redemp-tion. It was, though, up to the more fortunate to bring succour and relief to the sufferers and so to practise charity and gain in the process their own share of salvation. The presence of the poor was therefore God's gift to every-body else: an occasion to practise self-sacrifice, to live a virtuous life, to repent sins and to earn heavenly bliss. One can almost say that a society which sought the meaning of earthly life in life after death would need to invent another vehicle of personal salvation, were the poor not already at hand.

This was most certainly the case in the 'disenchanted' world, in which nothing that *was* had the *right to be* just because of the accident of being there, and in which everything that *was* had to show a legitimate and reasonable proof of its right to be. Most importantly, in contrast to pre-modern Europe, the brave new world of modernity was one that set its own rules and took nothing for granted, subjecting everything extant to the incisive scrutiny of reason, recognizing no limits to its own authority, and above all rejecting the 'power of the dead over the living', the authority of tradition, inherited lore or custom. The projects of order and the norm replaced the vision of a divine chain of beings. Unlike the vision replaced, order and norm were human products, designs yet to be implemented by human action – things yet to be made or built, not things found and placidly complied with. If inherited reality did not match the projected order, all the worse for reality.

And so the presence of the poor became a problem (a 'problem' is some-thing which causes discomfort and prompts the urge to resolve it, to remedy or remove it). The poor were a threat and an obstacle to order; they also defied the norm.

The poor were double jeopardy: since their proverty was no more the verdict of providence, there was no reason why they should humbly and gratefully accept their lot, but every reason for them to complain and to rebel against the more fortunate, now blamed for their deprivation. On the other hand, the old Christian ethics of charity appeared now an intolerable burden, a drain on the nation's wealth. The duty to share one's good fortune with those who failed to curry fortune's favours was once a sens-ible investment in life after death, but it 'did not stand to reason', certainly not to the reasons of business of life here and now, on earth.

Soon a third threat was added to the other two: the poor who meekly accepted their plight as divine verdict and made no effort to extricate them-selves from their misery proved immune to the blandishments of factory work and refused to sell their labour once the meagre needs they grew to habitualize and perceive as 'natural' had been satisfied. The early decades of industrial society were plagued by a constant shortage of labour. The poor, satisfied with their lot, or resigned to it, were thus the nightmare of industrial entrepreneurs: they were immune and irresponsive to the inducements of regular wages and saw no reason why they should go on suffering the long hours of drudgery once they had enough bread to see them through the day. A vicious circle indeed: the poor objecting to their misery spelled rebellion or revolution; the poor reconciled to their miserable lot curbed and hampered the progress of industrial enterprise. Forcing the poor into perpetual factory labour seemed a miraculous way to square the circle.

And so the poor of the industrial era were redefined as the reserve army of labour. Employment, steady employment, employment leaving no room for mischief, had become a norm while poverty had been identified with unemployment – a breach of the norm, an abnormal state. Under the circumstances, the obvious prescription for curing poverty and nipping in the bud the twin threats to prosperity was to induce the poor, or force them if need be, to accept the lot of factory labour. The most obvious means to achieve this was, of course, depriving the poor of any other source of livelihood: accept the conditions on offer, however repulsive they might be and however deeply you might resent them, or forfeit all right to a helping hand. Strictly speaking, in such a 'no alternative' situation, the preaching of ethical duty would be superfluous; it was not on the moral impulses of the poor that the intention to bring them all onto the factory floor needed to rely. And yet the work ethic was viewed almost universally as a useful, perhaps indispensable medicine for the triple ailment of poverty, insufficient supply of labour and the threat of revolution. It was meant and hoped to be a sort of icing hiding from view the unappetising quality of the cake on offer. Promoting drudgery to the noble rank of moral duty would perhaps sweeten the tempers of those exposed to it while at the same time catering to the moral consciences of those who exposed them. Opting for the work ethic was made, of course, that much easier – indeed, obvious and natural – by the fact that the middle classes of the time were already converted to it and viewed their own life in its light.

Enlightened opinion of the time was divided, but on the point of the work ethic there was full agreement between those who saw the poor as a wild and obstinate beast to be tamed, and those who were guided in their thinking by ethics, conscience or compassion. And so on the one hand John Locke devised a comprehensive programme to weed out the 'debauchery' and 'sloth' to which the poor were naturally predisposed, by confining the children of the poor in pauper schools which would drill them into regular work, and their parents in workhouses where severe discipline, bare sustenance, forced labour and corporal punishment were the rule. On the other hand Josiah Child, who bewailed the 'sad, wretched, diseased, impotent, and useless' fate of the poor, similarly considered the task of 'setting the poor to work' as 'man's duty to God and Nature'.[4]

In a roundabout way, the conception of work as 'man's duty to God' put an ethical stamp on keeping the poor in the state of poverty. Widely shared was the opinion that since the poor tended to settle for little and would not strain themselves for the sake of more, wages must be kept to a bare minimum of subsistence, so that even when employed the poor would still need to live from hand to mouth and keep perpetually busy in order to stay alive. In the words of Arthur Young, 'every one but an idiot knows, that the lower classes must be kept poor, or they will never be industrious'. The learned economists of the time hastened to calculate that when wages are low, 'the poor labour more, and really live better' than if they receive high wages, when they indulge in idleness and riot.

Jeremy Bentham, the great reformer who encapsulated modern wisdom better than any other thinker of his time (his project was praised almost unanimously by contemporary learned opinion as 'eminently rational and enlightened'), went a step further and concluded that financial inducements of any kind are not reliable means to get the desired effects; bare coercion would be much more effective than any appeal to the obviously fickle or absent intelligence of the poor. He proposed to build 500 houses, each to keep 2000 of the 'burdensome poor' under the constant surveillance and absolute, undivided authority of a governor. 'The refuse, the dross of mankind', adults and children without visible means of support, beggars, unwed mothers, unruly apprentices and the like should be, according to the scheme, apprehended and forced into such privately owned and run houses of compulsory labour, where 'the dross of this kind will be converted into sterling'. To his few liberally-minded critics Bentham replied angrily: 'Objection – liberty infringed. Answer – liberty of doing mischief'. He believed that the poor, just by staying poor, had given all the proof needed that they were no more capable of liberty than unruly children. They could not govern themselves; they had to be governed.

Much water has flowed under all sorts of bridges since people like Locke, Young or Bentham, with all the daring ardour of the explorers of new and unfamiliar lands, proclaimed what was to entrench itself gradually as the universally-accepted modern philosophy of the poor. Few people today would risk stating the principles of that philosophy with a similarly arrogant candour, and if they did, their assertions would certainly cause an outcry. And yet much of that philosophy informs once more much of the public policy regarding the people incapable, for one reason or another, of making ends meet and earning their living without 'unearned' assistance. One hears today a powerful echo of that philosophy in every successive campaign against 'spongers', 'cheaters' or 'dole dopes', and in every oft-repeated warning that people asking for better wages risk 'pricing themselves out of a job'. The impact of that philosophy is most strongly felt in the stubborn insistence, in spite of the massive evidence to the contrary, that breaking the norm of universal work-for-living is now, as before, the prime cause of poverty and that the cure for poverty must be sought in leading the unemployed back to the labour market. In the folklore of public policy, only as a commodity may labour claim the right of access to equally commodified means of survival.

And so the appearance is created that the poor of today have retained the function assigned to them in the early years of the new, modern and industrial, era – that of the reserve army of labour. The assignment of this function casts doubt and suspicion on the probity of those 'not in active service', and points clearly to the way to 'bring them back into line' and so restore the order of things which the avoidance of active service has broken. The snag, however, is that the philosophy which once tried to grasp and articulate the emerging realities of industrial age has by now outlived its purpose and lost touch with the new reality emerging at the other end of that age. Once an agent of the order-making effort, that philosophy turned slowly yet relentlessly into a smokescreen, obscuring whatever is new and unprecedented in the present plight of the poor. The work ethic, which casts the poor in the role of the reserve army of labour began its life as a revelation; it leads its posthumous life as a cover-up.

Grooming the poor of today into the labourers of tomorrow used to make sense economically and politically. It lubricated the wheels of the industry-based economy and served well the task of 'social integration' – that is, of order-maintenance and normative regulation. Neither of the two senses holds any more in our 'late modern' or 'post-modern', yet above all consumer, society. The present-day economy does not need a massive labour force, having learned how to increase not just profits, but the volume of products while cutting down on labour and its costs. At the same time, obedience to the norm and 'social discipline' in general are by and large secured through the allurements and seductions of the commodity market, rather than through the state-managed coercion and the drill administered by the network of panoptical institutions. Economically and politically, the late modern or post-modern society of consumers can thrive without dragging the bulk of its members through the millstones of industrial labour. For all practical intents and purposes, the poor have ceased to be the reserve army of labour, and invocations of the work ethic sound increasingly nebulous and out of touch with the realities of the day.

Contemporary society engages its members primarily as consumers; only secondarily, and partly, does it engage them as producers. To meet the social norm, to be a fully-fledged member of society, one needs to respond promptly and efficiently to the temptations of the consumer market; one needs to contribute to the 'supply-clearing demand' and in case of economic trouble be part of the 'consumer-led recovery'. All this the poor, lacking decent income, credit cards and the prospect of a better time, are not fit to do. Accordingly, the norm which is broken by the poor of today, the norm the breaking of which makes them 'abnormal', is the norm of consumer competence or aptitude, not that of employment. First and foremost, the poor of today are 'non-consumers', not 'unemployed'; they are defined in the first place through being flawed consumers, since the most crucial of the social duties which they do not fulfil is that of being active and effective buyers of the goods and services the market offers. In the book-balancing of a consumer society, the poor are unequivocally a liability, and by no stretch of imagination can they be recorded on the side of present or future assets.

And so for the first time in recorded history the poor are now purely and simply a worry and a nuisance. They have no merits which could relieve, let alone counterbalance, their vices. They have nothing to offer in exchange for the taxpayer's outlays. They are a bad investment, unlikely ever to be repaid, let alone bring profit; a black hole sucking in whatever comes near and spitting back nothing, except, perhaps, trouble. Decent and normal members of society – the consumers – want nothing from them and expect nothing. The poor are totally useless. No one – no one who truly counts, speaks up and is heard – needs them. For them, zero tolerance. Society would be much better off if the poor just burnt their tents and left. The world would be that much more pleasant without them. The poor are not needed, and so they are unwanted. And because they are unwanted, they can be, without much regret or compunction, forsaken.

No role, no moral duty

In a world populated by consumers there is no room for a welfare state; that venerable legacy of industrial society looks suddenly much like a 'nanny state', pampering the slothful, coddling the wicked, abetting the corrupt.

Some say that the welfare state was a hard-won achievement of the poor and lowly; if it was indeed the struggle of the poor and disprivileged that forced the hands of Bismarck, Lloyd George or Beveridge, that struggle could achieve its effect only because the poor had a lot of 'bargaining power' – they had an important function to perform, they had something vital and indispensable to offer to the society of producers. Apart from anything else, the welfare state was the means of recommodifying labour, making it sellable and purchasable in the first place and then again when temporarily slack demand for labour picked up once more. The state took that task on its shoulders, since the capitalists were unwilling or unable to carry the costs of that recommodification on theirs – singly, severally or jointly. Considering the double (economic and political) task that industrial employment performed, the welfare state, in meaning to make the idle work again, was under the circumstances a sound, profitable investment. But not any more. Making everybody a producer is neither feasible nor seems to be imperative. What used to be a sensible investment now looks more and more like a wrong-headed idea, an unjustifiable waste of taxpayers' money.

Not surprisingly, the welfare state is in retreat virtually everywhere. The few countries where its provisions are yet intact or its dismantling is slow or half-hearted are alternately reproached or ridiculed for their imprudence and obsoleteness by the chorus of current economic authorities, and warned by the economic sages and world banking institutions, as, for example, Norway repeatedly is, against the impending 'overheating of their economy' and other freshly invented horrors. The post-communist countries of East- and Central-Europe are told in no uncertain terms that the taking apart of inherited social protections is the condition *sine qua non* of any foreign assistance and, indeed, of acceptance into the 'family of free nations'. The sole choice brandished in front of governments by current economic wisdom is the quasi-choice between fast rising unemployment, as in Europe, and an even faster fall in the income of the lower classes, as in the USA.

The United States are taking the lead in this new welfare-free world. In the last 20 years, the total income of the 20 per cent poorest American families fell by 21 per cent, while the total income of the 20 per cent richest rose by 22 per cent.[5] Redistribution of income from the poorest to the richest goes on with unstoppably accelerating speed. Recent draconian cuts in welfare entitlements supported eagerly by threequarters of the elected members of Congress ('the end to welfare state as we know it', in the words of Bill Clinton) are bound to increase the number of American children growing up in poverty, between now and the year 2006, by 2 to 5 million, as well as multiply the numbers of the aged, sick and disabled deprived of any social assistance. In Loïc Wacquant's assessment, the purpose of American social policy is no longer to push back poverty, but to deflate the numbers of the poor (officially so recognized and thus eligible for help): 'The nuance is significant; just like once upon a time a good Indian was a dead Indian, so today the "good poor" is an invisible poor, who cares for himself and does not ask for anything. Briefly, someone who behaves as if he did not exist . . .'.[6]

It may be supposed that if they tried to defend whatever has remained of the protective shield forged by welfare legislation, the poor would soon find out that they have no bargaining power to make themselves audible, still less to impress their adversaries. Least of all would they find power to shake the 'ordinary citizens' out of their serene equanimity, exhortated as they are by the chorus of politicians to vote with neither mind nor heart but their wallets.

There is little chance of this supposition ever being put to the test, however. The poor do not seem to mind their plight, and if they do, there is little practical evidence of their anger or of determination to act on that anger. They suffer no doubt just like the poor of all ages suffered, but unlike their fathers and grandfathers they either fail or do not try to reforge their suffering into a matter of public concern. As Xavier Emmanuelli explained recently this astounding placidity of the poor:

Obviously, the 'classic' poverty, inherited from the past, transmitted from one generation to another, persisted in spite of the powerful economic growth in the industrialised country . . . But to that a new phenomenon is added, peculiar to our time of rapid change and unprecedented in its volume.

This is the accumulation, the linking of the reverses of fortune, which hurl individuals or whole families into destitution and often into the street: loss of employment, loss of income, bereavement, divorce, separation, loss of lodgings. From that chain exclusion results – isolation from the network of social interactions and exchanges, absence of reference points, inability to project one's lot into the future. This is why people called these days 'the excluded' do not come forward with demands or projects, do not come to value their rights, do not exercise their responsibilities as humans and as citizens. As they stopped to exist in the eyes of others, so they gradually stop to exist in their own eyes.[7]

These days the sufferings of the poor do not add up to a common cause. Each flawed consumer licks his or her wounds in solitude, at best in the company of their as yet unbroken family. Flawed consumers are lonely, and when they are left lonely for a long time they tend to become loners; they do not see how society can help, they do not hope to be helped, they do not believe that their lot can be changed by anything but football pools or a lottery win.

Unneeded, unwanted, forsaken – where is their place? The briefest of answers is: out of sight. First, they need to be removed from the streets and other public places used by us, the insiders of the brave new consumer world. Better still, if they happen to be fresh arrivals and have their papers in less than perfect order, they can be deported, and so evicted altogether from the realm of all obligation. If an excuse for deportation cannot be found, they may still be incarcerated in far-away prisons or prison camps, best of all in the Arizona desert, on ships anchored far from sailing routes, or in high-tech, fully automated jails where they see no one and no one, even the prison guards, is likely to meet them face to face very often.

To make the physical isolation foolproof, one can reinforce it with mental separation, resulting in the poor's banishment from the universe of moral empathy. While banishing the poor from the streets, one can also banish them from the community of humans, from the world of ethical duty. This is done by rewriting the story from the language of deprivation to that of depravity. The poor supply the 'usual suspects' rounded up to the accompaniment of public hue and cry whenever a fault in the habitual order is detected. The poor are portrayed as lax, sinful and devoid of moral standards. The media cheerfully cooperate with the police in presenting to the sensation-greedy public lurid pictures of the crime-, drug- and sexual promiscuity-infested 'criminal elements' who find their shelter in the darkness of mean streets. And so the point is made that the question of poverty is, first and foremost, perhaps solely, the question of law and order, and one should respond to it in the way one responds to other kinds of law-breaking.

Exempt from human community, exempt from public mind. We know what may follow when this happens. The temptation is strong to get rid altogether of a phenomenon reduced to sheer nuisance and unredeemed, not even mitigated, by any ethical consideration that is due to the suffering Other; to wipe out a blot on the landscape, to efface a dirty spot on the otherwise pure canvas of an orderly world and normal society. Alain Finkielkraut reminds us, in his recent book, of what might happen when the ethical considerations are effectively silenced, empathy extinguished and moral barriers taken away:

> Nazi violence was committed not for the liking of it, but out of duty, not out of sadism but out of virtue, not through pleasure but through a method, not by unleashing of savage impulses and abandonment of scruples, but in the name of superior values, with professional competence and with the task to be performed constantly in view.[8]

And that violence was committed, let me add, amidst a deafening silence from people who thought themselves to be decent and ethical creatures yet saw no reason why the victims of violence, who long ago ceased to be counted among the members of the human family, should be targets of their moral compassion. To paraphrase Gregory Bateson, once the loss of moral community is combined with the advanced technology of tackling whatever is seen as a vexing problem, 'your chance of survival will be that of a snowball in hell'[9]. Rational solutions to vexing troubles, when coupled with moral indifference, make indeed an explosive mixture. Many human beings may perish in the explosion, yet the most prominent among the victims is the humanity of those who escaped the perdition.

We are not quite there – not yet. But the writing is on the wall. Let us not dismiss it as one more prophecy of doom, normally forgotten long before tested, lest we need to follow once more the present fashion of retrospective, and belated, apology for not noticing it when it was still what it is today: merely writing on the wall. Luckily for mankind, history is strewn with portentous prophecies which failed to become flesh. But many, and the most heinous, crimes occurred in that history due to a lack of warning or thanks to the complacent incredulity with which any warnings were treated when heard. Now, as always in the past, the choice is ours.

Ethic of work or ethic of life?

And there is a choice; though one may expect that with realities notorious for their tendency to hide their human origins and assume the air of self-evident necessities, many people will dismiss any alternative to the present-day drift as 'irrealistic' and even 'against the nature of things', whatever they may mean by that. Imagining the possibility of another way of living together is not a strong point of our world of privatized utopias, known for its inclination to count losses when already made and for substitution of crisis management for political vision. Even less is this world of ours capable of gathering the will and resolve needed to make any alternative to 'more of the same' realistic. The dismissive label 'irrealistic', used and abused so widely in current political skirmishes, denotes primarily the *absence* of will and resolve.

As Cornelius Catoriadis pointed out recently, the crisis of the Western world 'consists precisely in the fact that it *stopped putting itself in question*'.[10] But 'putting itself in question' was the innermost secret of that Western world's astonishing, unprecedented quest for self-improvement and equally amazing success in the pursuit of that ever more ambitiously set objective. 'Putting itself in question' was possible – indeed inevitable – since the discovery that the foundations of all our arrangements are arbitrary and bound to stay as such. Being arbitrary, they may as well be replaced with other arrangements, if only the case for such a replacement could be convincingly made. This condition does not seem to be met any more, though. We tend to forget that 'to treat a person as a thing or as a purely mechanical system is not less but *more* imaginary than claiming to see him as an owl'. And once this is forgotten, we stop asking the sort of questions which used to make modern society the most restless and innovative of all. For example: 'everything is actually subordinated to effectiveness – but effective for whom, in view of what, and in order to do what? Economic growth is realised; but this is the growth of what, for whom, at what costs, and to arrive at what?'

With such questions not asked, there are no obstacles to the elevating of our own imaginary, incessant, on-going, tolerating, no limits rationalization (which rebounds in the replacement of a human person 'by an ensemble of partial features selected arbitrarily in terms of the arbitrary system of ends') to the rank of objective necessity and to make all doubts the exlusive domain of 'unserious people like poets and novelists'.[11]

A cogent and powerful case for a radical solution to the present crisis was presented recently by Claus Offe.[12] The hub of that solution is 'the idea that *individual income entitlement can be decoupled from actual income-earning capacity*'. It can, though admittedly on condition of no lesser a feat than a change of perspective from one centered on wage labour, as dictated by the work ethic, to the assumption of basic entitlement and basic guarantee, dictated by the status and dignity of being human:

> Decoupling is given concrete form by the principle of financing social security through taxation, through doing away with means-testing and assessment of willingness to work, by the gradual replacement of the principle of equivalence by that of need, and finally through the principle of the individual as the basis for entitlement. By transforming the social security system according to these principles, it is possible to carry over welfare state values of freedom, equality, and social justice into the phase of development which capitalist welfare states have now entered, a phase in which the goal of full employment has receded beyond the horizon of what is realistic and desirable.

Offe's proposals do sound nebulous, as could only be expected in the light of what had been said before about our growing inability to put our world in question. They could not sound otherwise at a time when every single political force that counts on the electoral market seems to run in an exactly opposite direction, and view the symptoms of disease as signs of recovery and the causes of disease as remedies. There seem to be no significant and organized political force on either the left or the right of the political spectrum which would not be inclined to dismiss Offe's and similar ideas on account of political expedience and electoral gains, though if pressed in public, 'responsible politicians' would probably dismiss the project of basic guarantee on the ground of its actuarial unaffordability or political and economic 'irrealism', glossing over the dubious realism of the presently fashionable crisis-management expedients.

And yet, as Offe rightly points out, his proposals are in the last account conservative. They suggest not a revolution, but the preservation of ethical values and social arrangements constitutive of Western civilization under conditions in which the inherited institutions no longer guarantee their implementation. And because the proposals have such conservative purpose,

> the burden of proof falls to [their] opponents . . . Either they wish to put an end to the postwar social ethical consensus, or they must show that their demands can be met in the long term by means *other* than that of a basic income – something which . . . seems to us highly doubtful.

It seems that Offe undervalues the opponents' resistance capacity by playing down the quite real possibility, supplied by the consumer society, of their choosing, against all imaginable odds, to 'put an end to ethical and social consensus'. Offe presents as a rhetorical question what is in fact quite a genuine practical dilemma. But whatever the chances are of the right choice being made, the choice is nevertheless as Offe describes it. The social and ethical consequences of barring its serious consideration by denying its presence are, purely and simply, incalculable.

However radical Offe's postulate may be, it still needs to be supplemented by another: that of the decoupling of work from the labour market. Melissa Benn recently observed that 'when male politicians talk about work, they almost inevitably mean paid work'.[13] This is not exactly true, since 'paid work' is on the mind of male and female politicians alike when they speak of work. Politics remains by and large male business, even if women are the players. What is true is that the identification of work with paid work has been historically the achievement of men who, as Max Weber indicated long ago, set their business away from the household, in which they left their women to perform all other necessary life activities, now no longer seen as work and so 'economically invisible'.

It is in this form that the idea of work entered politics, where it became the object of struggle on the similarly male-only playground – the battlefield of trade union rights and labour legislation. In this way, 'work' came to be confined to the kind of activity which can be entered into business books; that is, the kind of work which can be sold and bought, has an exchange value recognized in the market and so can command monetary

remuneration. Outside the realm of work was thereby left virtually everything which was cast as the exclusive domain of women – but not only
that. Whenever one spoke of work, one did not have in mind household
chores or the bringing up of children, both blatantly female provinces; but
also, more generally, one did not mean the myriads of social skills deployed,
and the endless hours spent, in the day-to-day running of what A.H. Halsey
and Michael Young call the 'moral economy'. The work ethic chimed
in with concentrated and unchallenged discrimination: staying outside the
labour market, doing unsold or unsellable labour, meant in the language of
the work ethic being unemployed, and that meant nonwork. Ironically, it
is only the high-level politicians who are allowed to declare publicly their
satisfaction when, having lost their jobs, they prepare to 'spend more time
with their families'.

The consequences of all this are in many respects disastrous. They contribute heavily to the gradual yet relentless falling apart of community and
neighbourhood bonds, of that 'social cohesion' whose maintenance is after
all a tremendously time-, labour- and skill-consuming activity. They leave
profound and by and large adverse traces on the structure and viability of
families. They seriously erode the soil in which the whole network of
human relationships and the moral bonds between people are rooted. All in
all, they have done and go on doing a lot of damage to the quality of life
(hardly ever distinguished from the 'standard of living', an altogether different matter), damage which no market offerings, no growth in consumer
capacity and no amount of counsellor advice can compensate or repair.

The emancipation of work from market-centred calculations and the
constraints they impose would require the replacement of the work ethic,
shaped in the service of the labour market, with an ethics of workmanship.
As Thorstein Veblen pointed out a long time ago, 'instinct of workmanship' (unlike the work ethic, a modern invention) is the natural predisposi-
tion of the human species. Humans are creative beings, and it is demeaning
to suppose that a price tag is what sets apart work from nonwork, exertion
from loafing; it mutilates human nature to suggest that without that price
tag humans would prefer to remain idle and let their skills and imagination
rot and rust. The ethics of workmanship would restore to that human
instinct the dignity and socially recognized significance which the work
ethic, as formed and entrenched in modern capitalist society, denied.

Not for the first time in history we have found ourselves on the crossroads. Crossroads call for decisions about which way to go, but the first,
crucial, and not at all obvious decision to be taken is to recognize the crossroads as a crossroads – to accept that more than one way leads from here
into the future, and that sometimes pursuing the future – any future – may
require sharp turns.

It is tempting to dismiss the idea of decoupling income entitlement from
income-earning capacity, and work from the labour market, as another
utopia in history, often described contemptuously as the 'graveyard of
utopias'. Our age is the time of 'individual utopias', of utopias privatized,

and so it comes naturally (as well as being a fashionable thing to do) to deride and ridicule such projects which imply a revision of the options which are collectively put at the disposal of individuals.

And so the ideas given shape by Offe may well be thought undeserving of a second thought by any serious and realistic scholar. And with good reason. As Roger-Pol Droit has recently expressed it, 'reality is full like an egg. To the point of making it virtually impossible to escape its constraints. We believe them to be eternal – until they are effaced by history'.[14] And he goes on pointing out that in Pericles' Greece or Caesar's Rome it would be a tall order to think of a world without slave labour, much like it would be all but impossible to think of a world without monarchy in the times of Bossuet. How can we be sure, therefore, that an economy which is not a slave of markets is an incongruity and that rising inequality cannot be stopped? Droit concludes: 'Instead of arresting the progress of utopia, our times prepare perhaps the ground for its return. The more we repeat that politics has no room for dreams, the more the desire of a radically different world worms in'. Paul Ricoeur would certainly agree: it was he who suggested ten years ago that in our era blocked by seemingly invisible systems it is the utopia which becomes our major resource as the weapon against the closure.[15] And quite recently, having completed his survey of Latin American history, Fernando Ainsa suggested that rather than speaking of *u*-topia, a place which is nowhere, it would be more proper to speak of *pan*-topia: the space of everywhere.[16]

The idea of decoupling income entitlement from income-earning capacity is in fact anything but conservative. On the contrary, what follows from our reasoning is that it would take a very sharp turn indeed to implement it. It would involve resignation from quite a few sacrosant (all the more sacrosant for being unreflexive) assumptions about our present mode of life. That, for instance, efficiency is a good thing regardless of what it might serve and what might be its side effects in terms of human suffering. Or that whatever passes for 'economic growth', i.e. what can be presented statistically as 'more today than yesterday, more tomorrow than today', is good by itself, once more regardless of the damage done on the way to the human condition and to nature – that condition shared by all humanity.

To those who would respond that the sharpness of the turn required is in itself a clinching argument against taking it, one can only reply by quoting once more Cornelius Castoriadis. When asked by one of his interviewers, 'What do you want then? To change humanity?', Castoriadis replied: 'No, something much more modest: I want that humanity changes, as it has already two or three times'.[17]

There is some hope at least that humanity might achieve the same feat once more. After all, as Patrick Curry splendidly put it, 'collective voluntary simplicity is becoming the only positive alternative to collective immiseration'.[18]

Notes

Chapter 1

1 J.S. Mill *Principles of Political Economy*, vol. II, 4th edn, London: John W. Parker & Son, p. 337.
2 Quoted in S. Pollard (1963) Factory discipline in the industrial revolution, *The Economic History Review*, second series, 16 (1963–4): 254–71.
3 W. Bowden (1925) *Industrial Society in England towards the End of the Eighteenth Century*. London: Macmillan, pp. 274–5.
4 J.L. Hammonds and B. Hammonds (1966) *The Town Labourer 1760–1832* (first published in 1917). London: Longman, p. 307.
5 W. Lepenies (1986) Historisierung der Natur and Entmoralisierung der Wissenschaften seit dem 18. Jahrhundert, in A. Peisl and A. Mohler (eds) *Natur und Geschichte*, vol. 7. Munich: Schriften der Carl Friedrich von Siemens Stiftung, pp. 263–88.
6 B. Inglis (1971) *Poverty and the Industrial Revolution*. London: Hodder & Stoughton, p. 75.
7 Revolt of the workers, *Blackwood's Magazine*, vol. 52, 1842, pp. 646–7.
8 The claim of labour, *Edinburgh Review*, vol. 81, 1845, pp. 304–5.
9 P. Gaskell (1836) *Artisans and Machinery*. London: Frank Cass 1968, p. 78.
10 See M. Rose (1985) *Re-working the Work Ethic: Economic Values and Socio-Cultural Politics*. London: B.T. Batsford, p. 30.
11 B. Inglis, op cit., p. 408.
12 G. Himmelfarb (1984) *The Ideas of Poverty: England in the Early Industrial Age*. London: Faber & Faber, p. 193.
13 See his *Panopticon*, or the *Inspection House*, containing the idea of a new principle of construction available to any sort of establishment, in which persons of any description are to be kept under inspection, in B. Bentham (1843) *The Works of Jeremy Bentham*, vol. 4. Edinburgh: William Tait, pp. 40–126.
14 J.S. Mill (1836) On the definition of political economy; and on the method of investigation proper to it, in *Collected Works*, vol. IV. London: Routledge & Kegan Paul 1967, p. 321.

15 K. McClelland (1987) Time to work, time to live: some aspects of work and the re-formation of class in Britain, 1850–1880, in P. Joyce (ed.) *The Historical Meanings of Work*. Cambridge: Cambridge University Press, p. 184.
16 R. Sue (1994) *Temps et Ordre Social*. Paris: PUF. Sue calculates that since 1850 the average time spent in work systemically fell; by the time of writing it had reached a mere 14 per cent of waking life.
17 M. Rose, op cit., p. 79.

Chapter 2

1 M. Wolf (1997) Mais pourquoi cette haine des marchés?, *Le Monde Diplomatique*, June, p. 15.
2 M. Weber (1976) *The Protestant Ethic and the Spirit of Capitalism*, trans. T. Parsons. London: George Allen & Unwin, p. 181.
3 M.C. Taylor and E. Saarinen (n.d.) *Imagologies: Media Philosophy*. London: Routledge, Telerotics, p. 11.
4 R. Petrella (1997) Une machine infernale, *Le Monde Diplomatique*, June, p. 17.
5 For the distinction between cognitive, aesthetic and moral spacings, see Z. Bauman (1993) *Postmodern Ethics*. Oxford: Blackwell.
6 Xavier Emmanuelli (*Le Monde*, 15 April 1997, p. 11) ridiculed another, closely related optical illusion caused by the tendency to project the elitist interpretation onto the lifestyles of those further down the social hierarchy. A life of travelling, mobility and freedom from home constraints being a highly esteemed value among the affluent tourists, younsters break with their families and flock to big cities in search of 'something different'. They tend to be eulogized (or rather romanticized) for their courage and self-confidence, which are deemed to prepare them for life in a society which praises and rewards individual initiative (recall Norman Tebbit's 'on your bike'). 'Nothing is as false', says Emmanuelli, as the idea that the wanderings of the children of the poor 'are the travels of initiation', which enable the youngsters 'to find themselves'. Nothing has less in common with the 'stage of initiation' than this aimless and prospectless errancy. 'Nothing is more destructive'.
7 P. Kelvin and J.E. Jarrett (1985) *Unemployment: Its Social Psychological Effects*. Cambridge: Cambridge University Press, pp. 67–9.
8 Ibid., pp. 67–9.
9 S. Hutchens (1994) *Living a Predicament: Young People Surviving Unemployment*. Aldershot: Avebury, pp. 58, 122.
10 J. Seabrook (1988) *The Race for Riches: The Human Cost of Wealth*. Basingstoke: Marshall Pickering, pp. 163, 164, 168–9.
11 Quoted after the report by G. Lean and B. Gunnell, UK poverty is worst in the West, *Independent on Sunday*, 15 June 1997.

Chapter 3

1 'Public welfare' is the term suggested by Kirk Mann in his discussion of the distiction made by Richard Titmuss in 1955 between fiscal, occupational and social welfare. Pointing out that setting apart 'social welfare' from the other two 'is slightly misleading, because the other two elements are also obviously social', Mann proposes to replace it with *public welfare*. 'It is public', says Mann, 'in the sense that it is visible and in so far as the public (in general of course)

identify this element with the welfare state' (see K. Mann (1992) *The Making of an English Underclass: The Social Divisions of Welfare and Labour*, Buckingham, Open University Press, p. 13.) I am using here the concept of 'public welfare' in a sense somewhat different from the one proposed by Mann – as an idea generic to all, more specific, forms of collectively provided individual welfare – whatever form that provision takes and whatever is the institution charged with its administration.

2 I. Gough (1979) *The Political Economy of the Welfare State*. London: Macmillan, p. 11.

3 C. Offe (1984) *Contradictions of the Welfare State*. London: Hutchinson, pp. 152–3.

4 Sir W. Beveridge (1945) *Why I am a Liberal*, here quoted in E.K. Bramsted and K.J. Melhuish (eds) *Western Liberalism: A History in Documents from Locke to Croce*. London: Longman 1978, pp. 712 ff.

5 A. Deacon and J. Bradshaw (1983) *Reserved for the Poor: The Means Test in British Social Policy*. Oxford: Basil Blackwell & Martin Robertson, p. 1 ff. 42.

6 R.M. Titmuss (1968) *Commitment to Welfare*. London: Allen & Unwin, p. 143.

7 A. Deacon and J. Bradshaw, op cit., p. 65.

8 R. Boyson (ed.) (1971) *Down with the Poor*. London: Churchill Press, p. 5.

9 J.F. Handler and J. Hasenfeld (1991) *The Moral Construction of Poverty*. London: Sage, p. 16.

10 Z. Ferge and S.M. Miller (eds) (1987) *Dynamics of Deprivation*. Aldershot: Gower, p. 297 ff.

11 C. Offe (1996) *Modernity and the State: East, West*. Cambridge: Polity Press, p. 172.

12 M. Woollacott (1997) Bosses must learn to behave better again, the *Guardian*, 14 June.

13 D. Duclos (1997) La cosmocratoie, nouvelle classe planetaire, *Le Monde Diplomatique*, August, pp. 14–15.

14 S. Halimi (1997) Allocation, équité, égalité, *Le Monde Diplomatique*, August, p. 18.

15 This is, of course, as repeatedly pointed out by students of consumerism, an illusion, but an illusion that protects reality and without which the reality of the consumer market would not be able to function. In fact, the promise and the visibility of choice (even the standard Macdonald beefburger you can eat in several incarnations), appealing to the energetically cultivated love of choice, is deployed to attract prospective consumers to the market place where the range of choice is strictly fixed and constrained. Whatever choice consumers may make, they would never step beyond the choice on offer, and the choice on offer is not itself a matter of consumer choice. It is dictated by unchosen, unelected managers – global companies which come ever closer to monopolistic rule over consumer markets. As John Vidal ('Empire of burgers', the *Guardian*, 20 June 1997) discovered: 'in eight sectors, including cars, aerospace, electronics, steel, armaments and media, the top five corporations now control 50 per cent of the global market'. And he concludes: 'This power is no longer merely financial, but also cultural. It is beginning to dictate the fundamentals of life. Ten corporations now control nearly every aspect of the world's food chain. Four control 90 per cent of the world's exports of corn, wheat, tobacco, tea, pineapple, jute and forest products'.

16 Let us recall that one of the most effective charges made in the Western propaganda war against communist regimes was the lack of choice in the shops. Whether the consumers suffered hunger and want, or were provided with the necessities of life, did not matter. What mattered more than anything else was

not the availability or even the quality of medical services, but the denial of choice between doctors; not the costs and availability of schools or accommodation, but again the lack of ability to choose between them. The widespread objections against lack of 'consumer choice' seriously undermined the popular support for the otherwise unquestionably superb state-administered services in Scandinavian countries.

17 This and following quotations come from Martin Walker's article 'God Bless (white) America', the *Guardian*, 17 May 1997.
18 M. Woollacott (1997) Behind the myth of the self-made man, the *Guardian*, 17 May.

Chapter 4

1 J.F. Handler and Y. Hasenfeld (1991) *The Moral Construction of Poverty*. London: Sage, pp. 139, 196–7. According to the authors, in 1971 in the framework of WIN 2.7 million assessments were made, but only 118,000 actually enrolled, and of those only 20 per cent held the job for at least three months. The median wage was $2 per hour (p. 141).
2 *International Herald Tribune*, 3–4 August 1996.
3 C. Julien (1996) Vers le choc social, *Le Monde Diplomatique*, September.
4 Z. Ferge and S.M. Miller (eds) (1987) *Dynamics of Deprivation*. Aldershot: Gower, pp. 309–10.
5 H.J. Gans (1995) *The War against the Poor: The Underclass and Antipoverty Policy*. New York: Basic Books, p. 2.
6 As Gans points out, 'non-poor alcoholics can drink at home, and sometimes even on the job, but poor ones are often found in the gutter. Moreover, the morally dubious acts of the better-off frequently turn out to be perfectly legal, in accord with the "golden rule": people who own the gold make the rules' (Ibid., p. 4).
7 It does not matter that federal and local expenditure on all kinds of welfare amounted to less than $40 billion in 1992 – that is but 15 per cent of the post-cold-war annual defence budget and $10 billion less than the annual cost of the mortgage tax deductions, or just one sixth of the total sum budgeted for corporate subsidies and tax breaks for the rich. It does not matter either that 'weapon producers may be as dependent on the Pentagon as poor women are on welfare' (Ibid., pp. 82–4).
8 K. Auletta (1982) *The Underclass*. New York: Random House, p. xiii.
9 The language of most current American debate concerning the phenomenon of the underclass is much more in line with the uncompromising, no-stops rhetoric of Edward Banfield: 'The lower-class individual lives from moment to moment . . . Impulse governs his behavior, either because he cannot discipline himself to sacrifice a present for a future satisfaction or because he has no sense of the future. He is therefore radically improvident; whatever he cannot consume immediately he considers valueless. His taste for "action" takes precedence over anything else' (E. Banfield (1968) *The Unheavenly City: The Nature and Future of our Urban Crisis*, Boston, Little Brown, pp. 34–5). Let us note that the Banfield diatribe aimed at the 'underclass' sounds like a very accurate description of the 'ideal consumer' in a society of consumers. In this, as in most other discussions, 'underclass' serves as a dumping ground for the demons haunting the consumer's tormented soul.

10 Auletta's field research brought him too close to the objects of the standardized treatment not to notice how empirically faulty are the generalized labels and wholesale classifications. At the end of his book (K. Auletta, op cit.), which presents one long story of a power-assisted *unification* of the underclass, he states: 'The one great lesson I learned from my reporting among the underclass and the poor is that generalizations – bumper stickers – are the enemies of understanding. It is perilous to generalize about the "lower class" . . . or about "victims" . . . or about poverty being "virtually eliminated" . . . or about government being "the problem". From a height of thirty thousand feet, everyone and everything looks like an ant' (p. 317). Expectedly, such warnings went unheeded. In its journalistic, political and popular reception Auletta's study served as another reinforcement of the unified image of the underclass.

11 K. Auletta, op cit., p. xvi.

12 Ibid., p. 28.

13 L.M. Mead (1992) *The New Politics of Poverty: The Nonworking Poor in America*. New York: Basic Books.

14 Ibid., p. x.

15 Ibid., p. 12.

16 Ibid., p. 133.

17 Ibid., p. 145.

18 Ibid., p. 261.

19 P. Townsend (1993) Poverty in Europe, in Z. Ferge and S.M. Miller (eds) *Dynamics of Deprivation*. Aldershot: Gower, p. 73.

20 N. Christie (1993) *Crime Control as Industry*. London: Routledge.

21 H.J. Gans, op cit., p. 75.

22 R. Kapuściński (1997) *Lapidarium III*. Warsaw: Czytelnik, pp. 146 ff.

Chapter 5

1 The choice has nothing 'necessary' or 'inevitable' about it. Abstractly speaking, it is arbitrary and contingent – it could be made differently (this is, precisely, what allows us to speak of a 'choice'). The choice, though, as Cornelius Castoriadis puts it, expresses itself in the 'imaginary' which holds society in its grip, underlying the way in which members of that society think, and indeed are able to think, of themselves and the world they inhabit. Given the pre-reflexive, 'naturalized', matter-of-fact character of that 'imaginary', members do not perceive the choice as choice, and are not aware of the contingency of the mode of life which sets them apart from other societies. The strength of the grip is a direct reflection of the overwhelming 'obviousness' of the selected mode and thus also of the difficulty to think of one's own and all other societies in any other perspective than that of one's own 'imaginary'. For instance, we are unable, 'when we speak of the feudal domain, to pretend to forget the concept of economy, or to avoid categorizing as economic, phenomena that were not so for people of the period' (C. Castoriadis (1987) *The Imaginary Institution of Society*, trans. K. Blamey, Cambridge, Polity Press, p. 163).

2 Here quoted in Peter Kussi's (1993) translation *The Farewell Party*, Faber & Faber, p. 85.

3 C. Castoriadis (1997) Anthropology, Philosophy, Politics, trans. D.A. Curtis (lecture given in Lausanne in 1989), in *Thesis Eleven*, 49, pp. 103–4.

4 G. Himmelfarb (1984) *The Idea of Poverty: England in the Early Industrial Age*. London: Faber & Faber, pp. 25. 79 ff, 193.

5 According to Lynn Karoly, the economist of the Rand Corporation, quoted in *International Herald Tribune*, 30–1 March 1996.
6 L. Wacquant (1996) Quand le président Clinton 'réforme' la pauvreté, *Le Monde Diplomatique*, September 1996.
7 X. Emmanuelli (1997) La maladie du lien, *Le Monde*, 15 April.
8 A. Finkielkraut (1996) *L'Humanité perdue: Essai sur le XXᵉ siècle*. Paris: Seuil.
9 G. Bateson (1973) *Steps to an Ecology of Mind*. Palladin Books, pp. 436–7.
10 C. Castoriadis (1996) *La montée de l'insignificance*. Paris: Seuil, p. 64.
11 C. Castoriadis (1987) *The Imaginary Institution of Society*, trans. K. Blamey. Cambridge: Polity Press, pp. 157–60.
12 C. Offe (1996) *Modernity and the State: East, West*. Cambridge: Polity Press, pp. 210 ff.
13 M. Benn (1997) Yes, but is there a philisophy to welfare-to-work?, the *Guardian*, 2 June.
14 R.P. Droit (1997) L'utopie est dans les étages, *Le Monde*, 18 July.
15 See P. Ricoeur (1997) *L'idéologie et l'utopie*. Paris: Seuil.
16 See F. Ainsa (1997) *La Reconstruction de l'utopie*. UNESCO.
17 C. Castoriadis (1990) *Le monde morcelé*. Paris: Seuil, p. 100.
18 P. Curry (1997) *Defending Middle-Earth*. Edinburgh, Floris Books, p. 51.

Index